SAMURAI BATTLES

ALSO BY WILLIAM DE LANGE:

Miyamoto Musashi
Musashi: Fact & Fiction
The Real Musashi, I, II, III
Famous Samurai, I, II, III
The Remarkable History of the Yaggyū Clan
A Dictionary of Japanese Onomatopeoia
A Dictionary of Japanese Proverbs
A Dictionary of Japanese Idioms
An Encyclopedia of Japanese Castles
A History of Japanese Journalism
The Namamugi Incident
A Fool's Journey
A Fool's Return
Japanese Scrolls
Pars Japonica
Iaido

PUBLISHED IN THE SAME SERIES:

Samurai Sieges

SAMURAI BATTLES

THE LONG ROAD TO UNIFICATION

WILLIAM DE LANGE

For more on books by William de Lange visit:
www.williamdelange.com

First edition, 2020
Second edition, 2021
Third, revised edition, 2023

Published by TOYO Press
Visit us at: **www.toyopress.com**

ISBN 978-94-92722-232

CONTENTS

OKEHAZAMA

The year is 1554. Following the sudden death of his father, Nobuhide, followed by a fierce internal struggle, Nobunaga has emerged as the new leader of the Oda clan with his headquarters at Kiyosu Castle. Only twenty-seven years old, Nobunaga faces many challenges. He is surrounded by powerful warlords, always looking for ways to widen their territory. One of them,

Nobunaga at Kiyosu Castle

Oda Nobunaga was born on June 23, 1534. Named Kippōshi at birth, he was the oldest son of Oda Nobuhide, the master of Shobata Castle, just west of the present town of Nagoya. Nobuhide was the court's magistrate for the four southern districts in Owari, and gradually widened his sphere of influence through his martial skill and effective tactics.

When Kippōshi was born, Nobuhide's influence was waning, chiefly due to the powerful Imagawa, who constantly made inroads into Owari from their power base of Sunpu in the province of Suruga. By the time Kippōshi was fifteen, his father's health was already failing and one of the young warrior's first official tasks was to compose a votive tablet at the Atsuta Shrine praying for his father's recovery. Though Nobuhide's eldest son, Kippōshi had his clansmen deeply worried, for his behavior was anything like that of a future chieftain. Though extremely bright, already at a young age he stood out as a complete eccentric. He usually went dressed in a *kosode* tied together with a strand of rope, his hair tied up in an unruly knot of bristles. By then, he was already known by the nickname of Owari no Utsukemono, the Dunce of Owari. Yet it seems that despite Kippōshi's eccentricity, Nobuhide had already spotted his son's hidden talents. Somewhere in the early forties, when Kippōshi was in his early teens, he was appointed master of Nagoya Castle. And it is from there, that he daily visited the castle's Tenōbō Temple to religiously devote himself to his studies.

In 1546, at the age of thirteen (twelve by Western counting) the young master underwent his genpuku, his coming-of-age ceremony. Attended by the same counselors who stood by him at Nagoya Castle, he received his adult name of Nobunaga, the name that would strike such terror into the hearts of so many of his countrymen over the next decades.

The next year, dressed in a crimson hood and a riding haori, Nobunaga took part in his first battle. Over the next years, he fought one battle after the other, many of them against members of his own clan. Using a combination of bravery, treachery and cunning, he one by one eliminated the contenders, including his younger brother Nobuyuki, whom he had assassinated at Kiyosu Castle.

Kiyosu Castle

Imagawa Yoshimoto, has already made inroads into Owari. Exploiting Nobuhide's death, he has won the support of the Yamaguchi clan, who control the strategic castles of Narumi and Kasadera. With their help Yoshimoto hatches a plan to also capture Oodaka and Kutsukake castles, both situated south of the Tenpaku River, forming the Oda's first line of defense against an Imagawa invasion.

To counter the growing threat, Nobunaga decides on a bold course of action. He immediately lays siege to Kasadera Castle, recapturing it within a matter of days. Unable to do the same with the castles of Narumi and Oodaka, he erects a number of fortresses in the vicinity, thus cutting off their supply lines from the Imagawa heartland of Tōtomi. More craftily, he also resorts to counter-intelligence. The *Kōyō gunkan* describes how Nobunaga sets about collecting his former correspondence with those who have joined the Imagawa camp. Based on these, he sets his scribes to work to draft recently dated letters, carrying the forged signatures of his defected vassals, suggesting they are still in communication with him, and conspiring to set a trap for their new master, Imagawa Yoshimoto. These letters he allows to be intercepted by Imagawa spies. The ruse works and several of the hapless conspirators are ordered to commit *seppuku*.

Now it is Yoshimoto's turn to move. Riled by his vassals' apparently unceasing conspiratorial activities and thwarted by Nobunaga's blockade of Narumi and Oodaka castles, he decides to invade Owari and relieve his strongholds by force. Raising a force of some twenty-five thousand men, he departs from his headquarters at Sunpu (Sunpu Castle was erected only in 1585) on 5 June 1560 and marches westward. Crossing the border with Owari, he reaches Kutsukake Castle five days later. The next evening, June 11, during a lengthy war council with his generals, Yoshimoto decides to dispatch his seventeen-year-old general Matsudaira Motoyasu (who would later be known as Tokugawa Ieyasu) toward Oodaka Castle with provisions, while

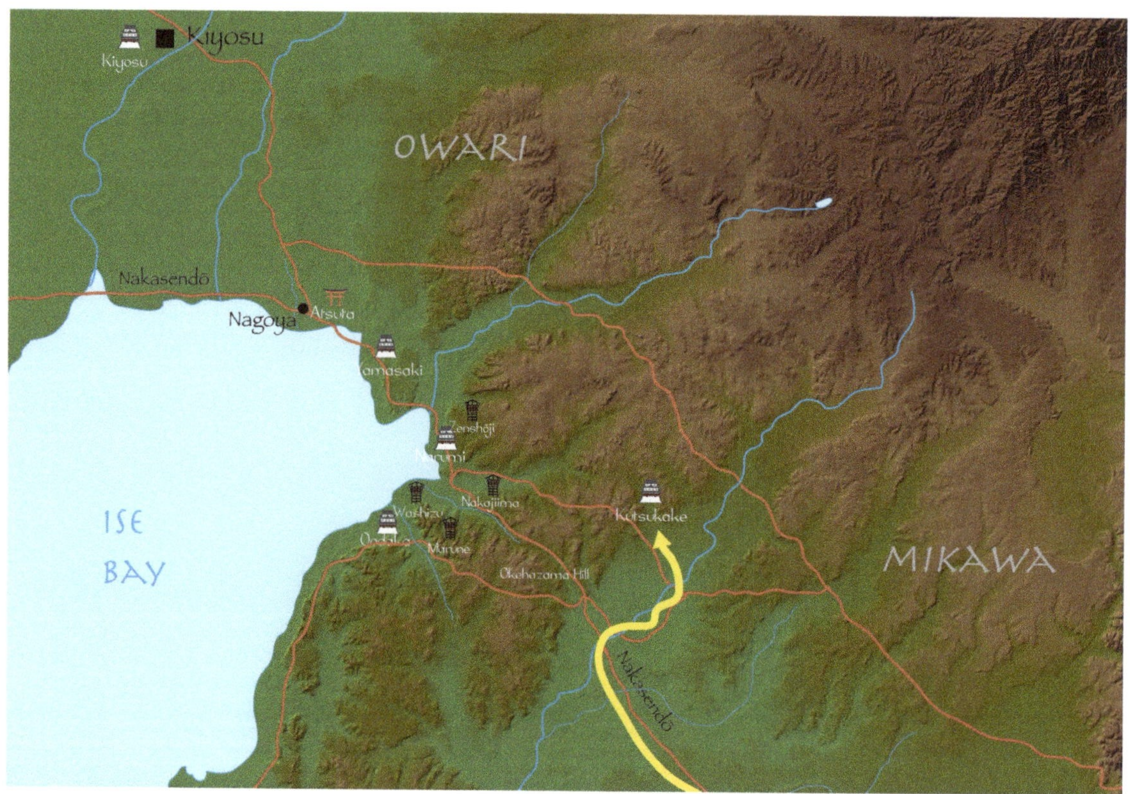

A young Motoyasu relieves the Imagawa warriors at Oodaka Castle

the rest of his force will attempt to lay siege, or at least attack Nobunaga's headquarters of Kiyosu Castle.

The *Shinchō kōki* describes how Nobunaga's spies inform him of the content of his enemies' war council. He seems unruffled and spends the night in empty banter, not ever once mentioning the enemy's movements, let alone convene a war council. Finally, around midnight, he laughs off the concerns of his counselors and tells them to go home as it is already late (*mō yoru ga fuketa, mina kitaku seyo*).

The next morning, 12 June, the young Motoyasu is the first to clash with Oda forces, when at the hour of the Ox (three o'clock in the morning) he attacks the makeshift strongholds of Marune and Washizu, which both face Oodaka Castle from across a small stream. Hearing of Motoyasu's attack, Nobunaga—who has not budged since word reached him of Imagawa's invasion—rises from his bed and acts out a scene from the popular play Atsumori: 'Man's life is but an illusion when compared to the after world' (*ningen gojūnen, keten no uchi wo kurabureba, mugen no gotoku nari*). Then he grabs some food, hoists himself into his armor, puts on his helmet, orders his generals to rally their men, and sets out from Kiyosu Castle with just five guards

The ancient Atsuta Shrine

on horseback. They arrive at the Atsuta Shrine at the hour of the Dragon (roughly eight o'clock in the morning). There Nobunaga offers prayers to the deities of war and waits for the arrival of his troops. By ten o'clock, some two to three thousand men have joined him.

Meanwhile, five hundred of Nobunaga's men are engaged in fierce hand-to-hand combat with Motoyasu's fearsome Imakawa warriors. Soon Nobunaga loses his first commander, Sakura Daigaku (Morishige), who falls together with the fortress of Marune. Things fare little better at the fortress of Washizu, where Nobunaga loses his granduncle, Hidetoshi. More importantly, Imagawa Yoshimoto has departed from Kutsukake Castle and is moving westward, apparently to join forces with those of Motoyasu.

Nobunaga and his men, by now, have reached the fortress of Zenshōji (not to be confused with the famous Zenshōji Temple). It is somewhere at this juncture that one of his scouts, Yanada Masatsuna, arrives with the news that Yoshimoto is spotted near Okehazama, some two miles south-east along the Tōkaidō. Part of his force has been kept behind at Kutsukake Castle to guard his rear. From his defeated men at Marune and Washizu Nobunaga knows that Motoyasu is still holding up at Oodaka Castle. This is a critical moment: the moment Yoshimoto and Motoyasu join forces he is doomed.

Yet even now, Nobunaga decides the odds are stacked too much against him. And thus he conceives of another ploy. The *Shinchō kōki* describes how Nobunaga orders three hundred of his men stationed at Zenshōji fortress to harass part of Yoshimoto's main force and lure them away from Okehazama. The ploy works. A large Imagawa contingent is sent in pursuit. Some fifty men of Nobunaga's decoy force lose their lives. Yet he has achieved his aim: by noon, a large part of Yoshimoto's force has been dispersed farther westward, near Takaneyama.

Nobunaga's ploy serves another purpose. Congratulating himself on his easy-won victory and far from impressed with his opponent's ability to muster sufficient forces, Yoshimoto sets up camp atop a shallow hill near

太平記英勇傳
今川治部大輔義元

Opposite page:
Imgawa Yoshimoto

Okehazama (Okehazama-*yama*, roughly 60 meters high), and enjoys a cup of *sake* with his generals to celebrate the positive turn events have taken: Motoyasu is in control of Oodaka Castle, and Nobunaga's petty vanguard has been taught a painful lesson. By now the sky has darkened and it has started raining heavily. With no further sign of hostilities, Yoshimoto's men settle down and wait for the clouds to lift.

Now Nobunaga is left with just one major hurdle. His men are still outnumbered two to one and the enemy occupies the high ground. He needs the advantage of surprise. Yet to do so he has to move his men closer to Okehazama-*yama*; to the makeshift fortress of Nakajima, halfway Zenshōji and Okehazama-*yama*. And thus he leaves behind five hundred men at Zenshōji with all his battlefield banners. These they are to raise shortly after his departure, suggesting to the enemy that his whole force is still gathered at Zenshōji. Then, making good use of the increasing rain, he and the remainder of just over two thousand set off towards Nakajima.

Arriving safely at the Nakajima fortress, Nobunaga waits for another agonizing hour. The *Shinchō kōki* describes how, while they are waiting in the pouring rain, crouching among the undergrowth so as not to be spotted by the enemy, Nobunaga addresses his men:

> 'Now all of you listen up! The Imagawa warriors ate their last rations last evening and have spent the whole night carrying provisions to Oodaka Castle, fighting hard with our men at Washizu and Marume. They will be exhausted. We, on the other hand, are rested. Who knows not the saying "Do not fear a great enemy just because you have fewer men; victory or defeat are decided in heaven." When the enemy attacks, we withdraw; when they withdraw, we attack. Whatever the cost we must crush them. It is easy. Do not waste time in trying to wrest arms from your opponents. Simply cut them down. If only we win this one battle, those who are with me here today will see their prestige of their houses lifted till the end of days!'

Yoshimoto emerges from his tent

Finally, at one o'clock in the afternoon, while the rain is coming down thick and fast, Nobunaga and his warriors head straight for Okehazama-*yama*

Yoshimoto is pinned down by Mōri Shinsuke

and charge up the shallow hill. They completely surprise the enemy. Emerging from his tent, Yoshimoto at first believes his men are quarreling among themselves. By the time he realizes they are under attack, it is already too late, and before long his forces gradually begin to give way. Casting his helmet aside Yoshimoto tries to make his escape. But just a few hundred yards downhill, bogged down in the mud, he is pinned down by Nobunaga's elite guard under the command of Mōri Shinsuke Yoshikatsu, who takes Yoshimoto's head. The warlord's last act of defiance is to bite off one of Yoshikatsu's left-hand fingers.

Presented with Yoshimoto's head, Nobunaga ties it to his saddle and orders his men to retreat to Kiyosu: the battle is won; without their chieftain, the Imagawa will not have the stomach to go on. Later, safely back at Kiyosu Castle, Nobunaga holds a *kubi jikken*, an inspection of the severed heads of the enemy warriors. In all, his men have gathered close to three thousand heads from the field of battle. One of his retainers has captured alive a cleric who had been in charge of Yoshimoto's whip and archery glove. Nobunaga treats him cordially and tells him to recount his lord's last moments on earth and to point out the heads of the major players in this final tragic scene.

Maeda Toshiie, one of Nobunaga's generals, with the heads of enemy warriors

Then, ordering one of his pages to bring a brush and ink, he one by one reverently writes their names on their foreheads. The next day, he sends the monk on his way in the company of ten guards. He is to carry Yoshimoto's head back to his headquarters of Suruga, so he can have a proper burial—and to serve as a reminder of the fate that awaits those who would seek to step in his shoes.

Later still, during a *ronkōkōshō*, a formal occasion in which a chieftain rewards his retainers, Nobunaga stuns his clansmen by not awarding the main prize to Mōri Shinsuke Yoshikatsu, the warrior who has taken Yoshimoto's head. Instead, the main prize of Kutsukake Castle and three million mon goes to Yanada Masatsuna, the scout who provided him with the most vital piece of intelligence: the whereabouts of Imagawa Yoshimoto.

ANEGAWA

The effect of Nobunaga's victory at Okehazama is electrifying. Overnight he becomes one of the most celebrated warlords in the realm. His incredible feat of defeating an army six times the size of his own stuns his contemporaries, and he soon becomes known as the Foremost Daimyō of Owari.

Most impressed with Nobunaga's victory is Matsudaira Motoyasu (Tokugawa Ieyasu). Hearing of Yoshimoto's death, he immediately withdraws his troops to Mikawa. There he visits the Daiju-*ji*, his old family temple near Okazaki Castle. Retreating into the temple grounds, he prepares to commit *seppuku* in front of his ancestor's grave, when the temple's chief priest implores him to reconsider: 'Does not the Buddhist phrase go *Enri-edo kongu-jōdo*? "Abhor the impurity of this world; Seek rebirth in the Pure World." Yet, were you to pacify this wicked world while you are still in it; how much more would you enjoy the Buddha's divine protection!' Taking heart from the monk's words, Motoyasu installs himself in his clan's former castle of Okazaki, which has been abandoned by the Imagawa warriors following their lord's demise.

Motoyasu is now his own master, but he can no longer count on the backing of the Imagawa, as Yoshimoto's death has dealt a fatal blow to the once so powerful clan. The young chieftain has great faith in his Mikawa warriors, yet his Matsudaira clan is only small and being threatened from all sides by

The Daiju Temple, the place where Motoyasu contemplated his end

far more powerful clans: the Takeda from the north, and the Hōjō from the east, and the Uesugi beyond—he needs a new strong ally, and he needs one fast. So it is not long after the Battle of Okehazama that he turns to his former enemy, Oda Nobunaga.

With his rear covered by his new ally in Mikawa and his flank by an alliance of sorts with Takeda Shingen, Nobunaga feels confident to turn his attention westward, toward the capital. He is ready to take the next step in his new vision for Japan: *tenka fūbū*; to rule the entire realm. Needless to say, given Nobunaga's character, this is to happen by way of force. Yet this is not just a result of his own disposition. There are many forces fiercely jealous of any attempts toward centralized control. There are the Ikkō sectarians and various Buddhist sects, all vying for hegemony over the Japanese soul and the power it brings. And then there are the Ashikaga Shōguns, who have seen their power gradually slip away until, like the imperial house, they have become puppets in the hands of powerful warlords. The latter, too, are keen to at least maintain the status quo, if not grab more land for themselves.

To test their readiness to fall into line, Nobunaga sends around messengers, inviting them to attend a grand banquet to pay their respect to Ashikaga Yoshiaki, the new Shōgun he has only recently installed in the capital. Most duly comply. But not all. Asakura Yoshikage refuses to budge from his headquarters of Ichijōdani Castle in Echizen. This is remarkable since the Asakura have always been such stout defenders of the Ashikaga shogunate. Indeed, only a few years earlier, Yoshikage has given the Shōgun refuge and helped him to plan his return to the capital. But Yoshikage sees through Nobunaga's scheme: he may be happy to see the Shōgun reinstalled; he is far from happy to see him backed by the likes of Nobunaga.

And thus, on 23 June 1570, Nobunaga raises yet another large army, some thirty thousand men, to lay siege to Ichijōdani Castle. Departing from Kyoto, he camps at Wani, on the shores of Lake Biwa. From there he makes his way to Kanegasaki, where he reduces the castles of Kanegasaki and Tezutsuyama within a matter of days. With him rides his new ally Tokugawa Ieyasu, who

Motoyasu turning to his former enemy was not as strange at it might seem. When young, he spent two years at Atsuta as a hostage of the Oda clan. And it is believed that, during that time, Takechiyo, as he was then still called, first encountered the eccentric Kippōshi, who was ten years his senior. It is said that Kippōshi took a liking to Takechiyo, bringing him along on many of his eccentric adventures.

It might well have been through Katō Yorimori, the old Oda hand who looked after Takechiyo during his stay at Atsuta, that Motoyasu approached his former playmate. Nobunaga responded positively, and two years later, at Kiyosu Castle, the two men formally signed what came to be known as the Kiyosu Dōmei, the Kiyosu Alliance. Shortly afterward the alliance was sealed by the marriage of Nobunaga's daughter, Tokuhime, to Ieyasu's eldest son, Nobuyasu.

Nobunaga, on his side, would form many such pacts and truces with other warlords: the Saitō in Ōmi, the Takeda in Kai, the Matsunaga in Nara, but none of them would hold. Only his alliance with Ieyasu would remain intact, enduring for more than twenty years.

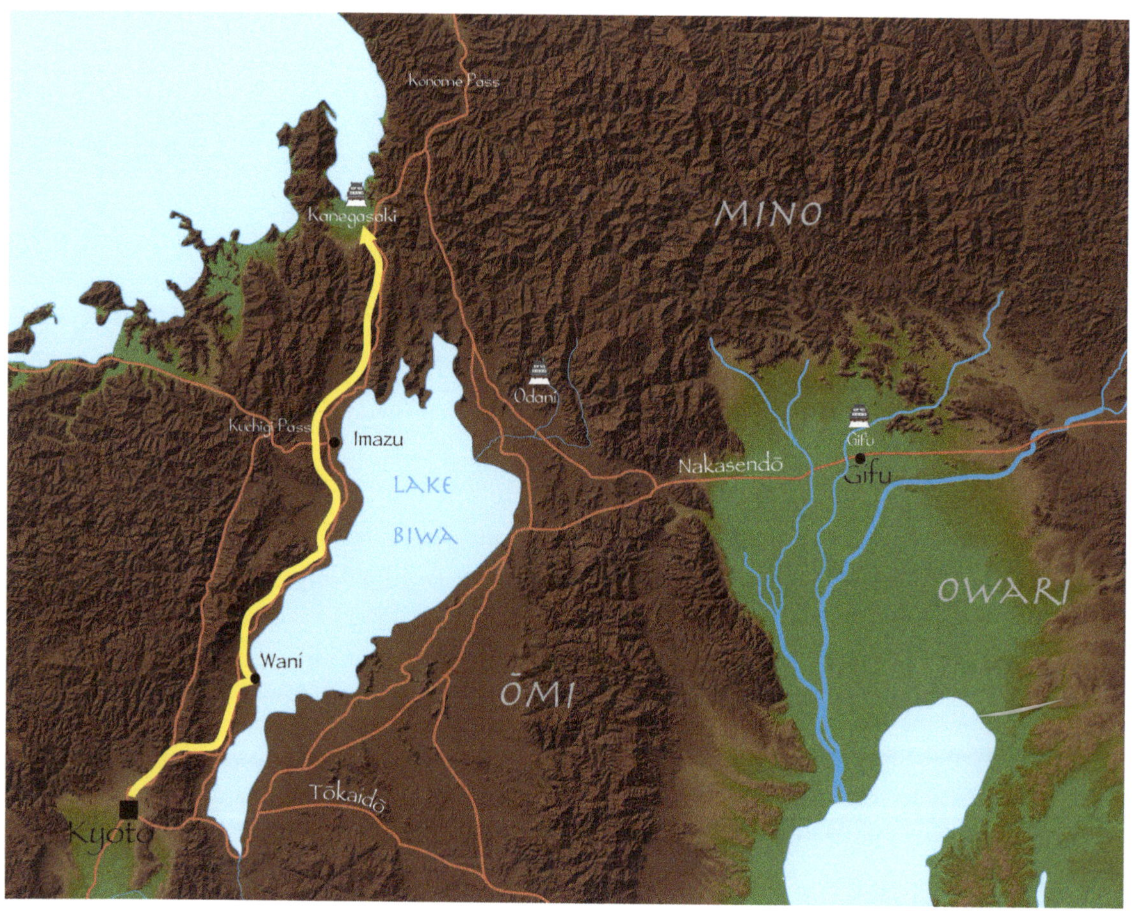

ten years before still fought him at Okehazma. To further pave the way, he has also forged an alliance with young warlord Azai Nagamasa, the master of Odani Castle, on the northeastern shore of Lake Biwa. Only twenty-five years old, Nagamasa has already conquered most of northern Ōmi, which borders on Echizen in the north. To bolster his new alliance, Nobunaga has married out to Nagamasa his sister, Oichi no Kata, equally known for her beauty as her fierce intelligence. Though one of convenience, it seemed theirs is a truly happy marriage. This is just as well, as the Azai and the Asakura have previously been close allies.

Nobunaga has just crossed the Konome Pass, the natural boundary between Ōmi and Echizen, when his scouts tell him that Azai Nagamasa has turned against him and is joining forces with his old ally, Asakura Yoshikage. At first, he dismissed it as 'mere rumors.' But when his sister sends him an embroidered bag that is sewn close on both sides—a clear hint that he is being trapped—has knows it is true. In a way the beautiful Oichi no Kata must feel trapped too. Though she has found bliss with her husband, their's is still a political marriage, and it is quite common for women to be returned to their original clan when such an alliance is severed.

Nobunaga's response is typical: '*Zehi ni oyobazu*' (Such is life). He leaves Ieyasu and his generals Hashiba (Toyotomi) Hideyoshi, and Akechi Mitsuhide behind to manage the retreat and vanished from the scene. Traveling through Wakasa and western Ōmi, he safely reaches Kyoto by way of the Kuchigi Pass. It is said that when he arrives, he is accompanied by no more than ten guards. Back in the capital, he acts as if nothing has happened. In truth, he

The Konome Pass

瓢軍談五十四場
十五
仙住坊

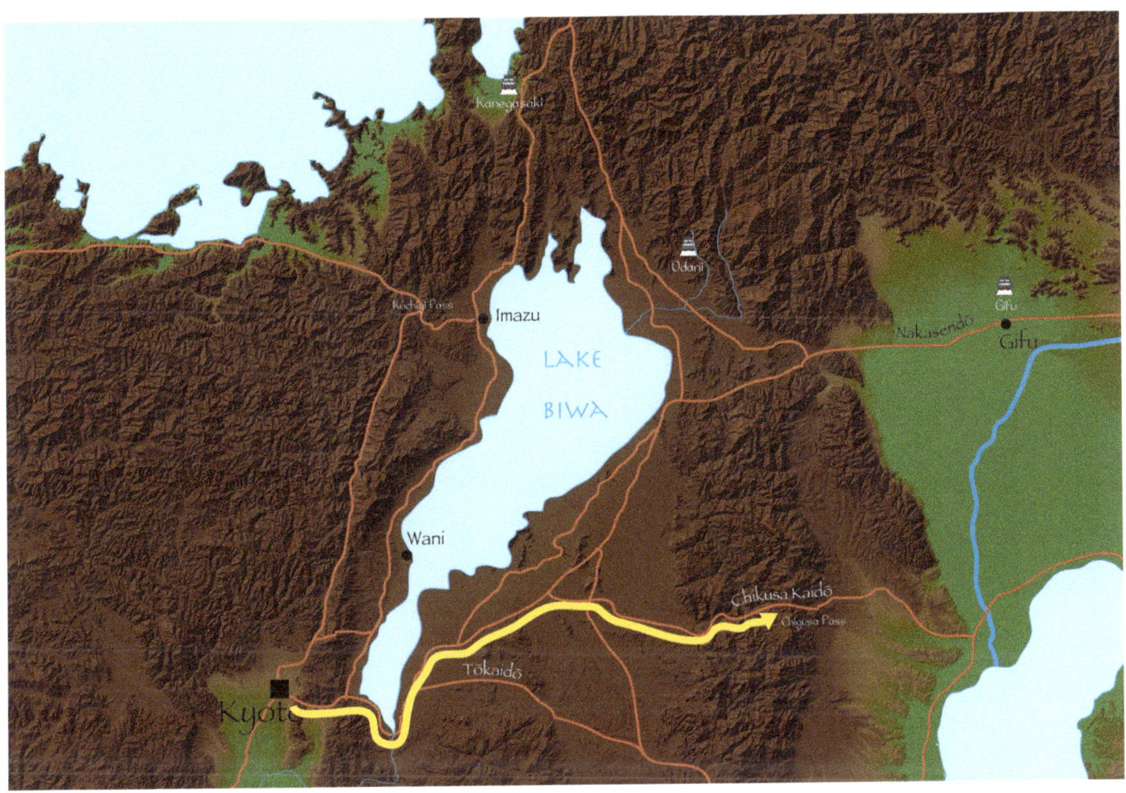

is seething with rage against his treacherous brother-in-law, who only weeks earlier graciously attended the grand banquet in honor of the Shōgun.

On July 21, Nobunaga is already on his way again, back to Gifu this time, to raise a larger army there. He is forced to take a detour along the Chikusa Highroad through Ise to avoid being intercepted by Nagamasa, or his allies, who still occupy castles along the Nakasendō. En route, he is shot at by Sugitani Zenjubō, a renowned marksman belonging to the Negoro sect, and who has been hired by the former governor (Rokkaku Yoshikata) of the province to assassinate Nobunaga in revenge for evicting him from his castle of Kannonji two years earlier. Twice Nobunaga is struck, but the bullets are fired from some distance (sixty yards), and fail to pierce his coat of armor.

Arriving back safely in Gifu two days later, Nobunaga raises an army of eighteen-thousand men and marches on Azai Nagamasa's headquarters of Odani Castle, reaching its vicinity on 23 July.

Opposite page: Sugitani Zenjubō takes carefull aim

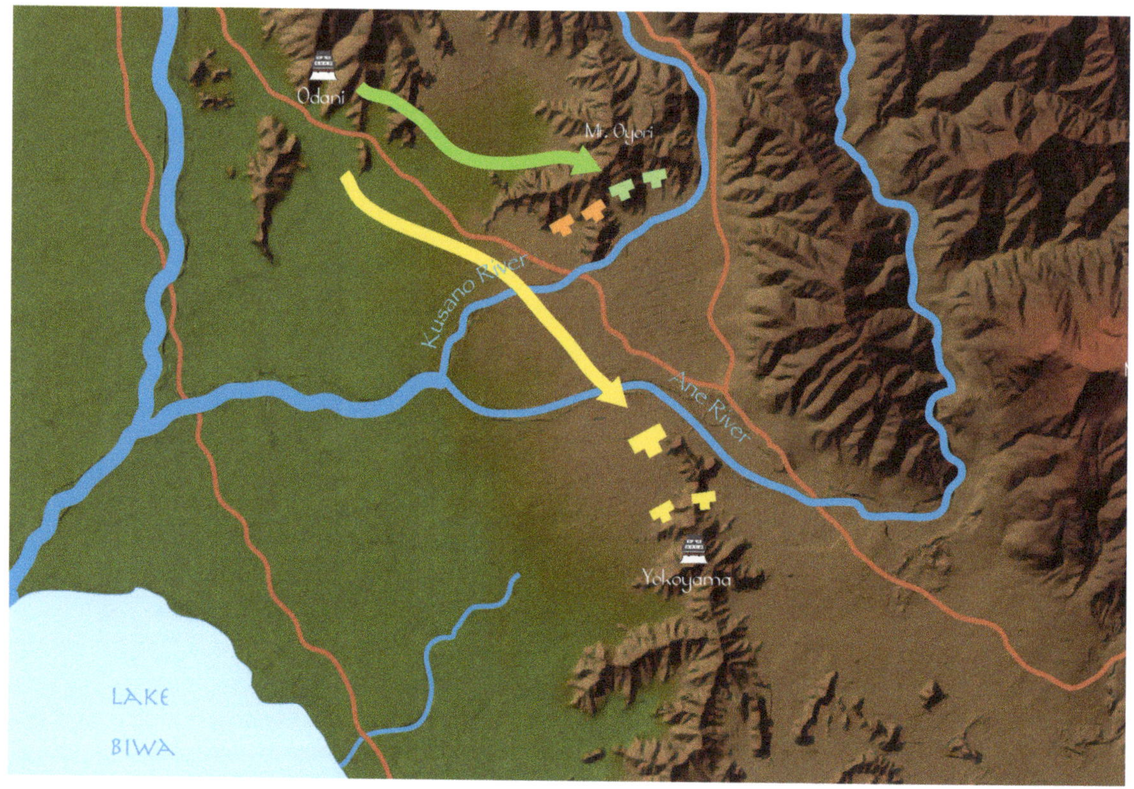

This time it is Asakura Yoshikage's turn to come to his ally's aid. Yet instead of showing up himself, he sends his cousin, Kagetaka. For the time being, Nagamasa is safe; sitting atop Mount Odani, his castle is reputed to be unconquerable—just like that of Ichijōdani, the stronghold of his ally.

Unwilling to needlessly sacrifice his men, Nobunaga resorts to his usual box of tricks, setting fire to local villages in an attempt to coax Nagamasa from his lair. But Nagamasa refuses to budge; he is still waiting for Yoshikage's reinforcements. And thus, on 26 July, Nobunaga crosses the Ane River and lays siege to the castle of Yokoyama, some five miles southeast of Odani Castle. This time Nobunaga does manage to coax his enemy from his lair. The next day, Nagamasa descends from his castle with a force of some five thousand men and takes up positions on the slopes of Mount Ōyori, just north of the Kusano River. Two days later, he is joined by eight thousand men under the command of Asakura Kagetaka, making their combined force thirteen-thousand men strong—almost half of that of Nobunaga, who has meanwhile been joined by his ally Ieyasu with some five-thousand men.

On the dawn of 29 July, Nobunaga is woken with the news that the enemy is on the move again. At first, it seems they are retreating. They descend from Mount Ōyori, cross the Kusano River, and are moving westward when they ground to a halt and take up positions along the northern bank of the Ane River. Nobunaga is taken by surprise, what should have been his vanguard is still posted at Yokoyama Castle, while his personal guard has now suddenly become his vanguard. Making do with the situation, he arranges his men thirteen ranks deep, so that they might the better absorb the enemy's assault. Bearing a particular grudge against his treacherous brother-in-law, Nobunaga insisted his troops face those of Nagamasa, leaving Ieyasu to deal with the much larger Asakura force.

Magara Jurōzaemon's challenge is met

Intense fighting erupts in the early hours of 30 July, when two of Ieyasu divisions cross the Ane River and engage the Asakura forces head-on. The Asakura and Azai men immediately responded in kind. The *Nobunaga-ki* describes how:

> In the thick of the fight, a mounted warrior from among the Asakura ranks by the name of Magara Jurōzaemon spurs on his horse, and, wielding around a five-foot longsword as if it were the wheel of a water mill, drives straight into the middle of the enemy ranks and calls out 'those who have the stomach come forward and fight me in hand to hand combat.' His challenge is met by two warriors, brothers, who step forward and announce their names and pedigree as custom requires. As they confront and size each other up, fighting around them ceases, and warriors of both camps watch with bated breath to see how the duel will end. One of the two lancers charges, thrusting his lance toward the mounted warrior, but the latter parries it with such force that the tip of the lance breaks off. The lancer, who loses his balance and lunges forward, is almost decapitated by the trajectory of the sword, which goes straight through the guards of his helmet.

The battle is in full swing

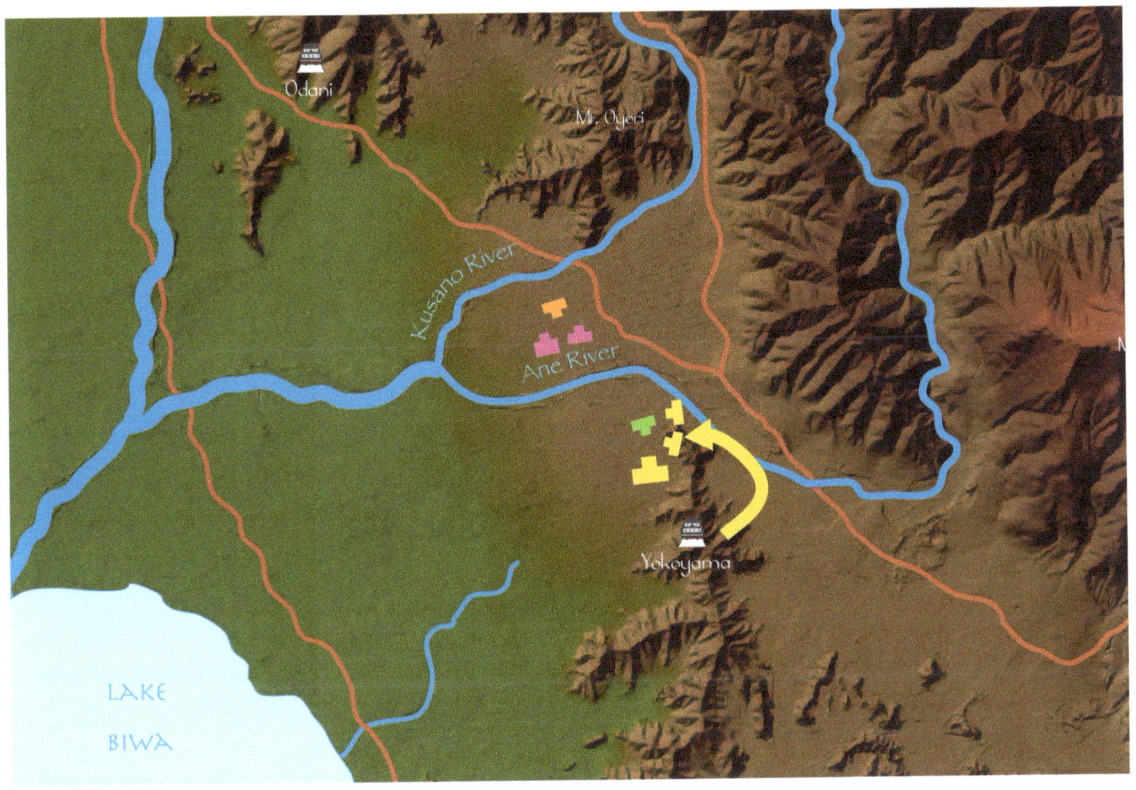

At this, his brother and a number of his retainers crowd in on the horseman and collectively thrust their weapons at Jurōzaemon breast. Wounded and feeling his life ebbing away the mounted warrior drops his head and speaks his last heroic words: 'Go ahead. Take my head and make it one of your feats.'

It is especially the Azai warriors who surprise Nobunaga with their ferocity. Fighting on home soil they risk everything to evict the enemy. They penetrate deep into the Nobunaga ranks, crushing one rank after another until only two out of thirteen hold their position. Nobunaga's rescue comes from his advance guard posted at Yokoyama Castle, which delivers a crushing blow on the left flank of the Azai. It is a decisive moment. Outnumbered and squeezed from all sides, the Azai begin to retreat toward the safety of Odani Castle, leaving the Asakura painfully exposed. At this the Asakura,

Azai Nagamasa

Oichi no Kata

One of the last things Nagamasa did, as he awaited the inevitable end, was to write a short letter (below) to Katagiri Genuemon Naosada, one of his most trusted retainers:

This time, unfortunately, all that remains is this castle's honmaru. Yet you have not chosen to join those who have fled the castle. Instead, you have remained steadfast in your resolve to defend and hold the castle, for which I am deeply grateful. Given that almost all have by now deserted, your conduct is unparalleled, something I cannot find the words to express in a letter. Your's sincerely, Azai Nagamasa.

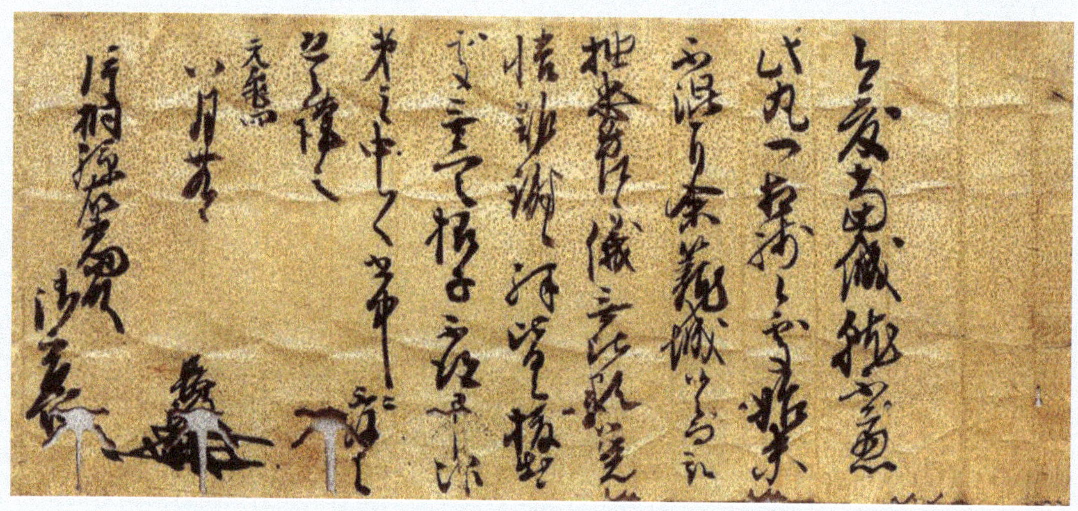

Old map of Odani Castle and its environs

too, begin to retreat, yielding to their opponents a victory that had almost been theirs. Had they been led by a more forceful commander they might have won the day, but neither Kagetaka, nor any of the other commanders under which they serve that day have the kind of boldness or grit of Ieyasu's Mikawa warriors.

In the end, it will take Nobunaga three more years to reduce the legendary Ichijōdani and Odani strongholds. Ichijōdani is the first to fall. It does so with its lord, who commits ritual suicide together with his family and clansmen. Next Nobunaga marches on Odani Castle, determined to do the same there. Before long his men have fought their way towards the castle's main tower. But then a remarkable thing happens: Nobunaga orders them to halt hostilities. Among those holding out inside is his beloved sister, Oichi no Kata. It seems that his love for his sister is matched by that of her husband. Refusing her offer to die alongside him, Nagamasa sends her and their children into the hands of his brother-in-law with the words: 'I want you to live and pray for my salvation once I'm dead.'

MIKATAGAHARA

The year is now 1572. Ieyasu is thirty years old. He has come a long way since his narrow escape in the wake of the Battle of Okehazama. He is now the master of Hamamatsu Castle, his new headquarters in his newly conquered province of Tōtōmi, and has prudently forged an alliance with his former foe, Oda Nobunaga. The latter, by now, has grown into one of the most powerful warlords in the realm. Building on his stunning victory at Okehazama, he has gone on to win battle after battle: Moribe (1561), Kōnoshima (1566), Inabayama Castle (1567), Kannonji Castle (1568), Okawachi Castle (1569), Kanegasaki Castle (1570), and Ane River (1570). It is Ieyasu's brilliant performance at Ane River that has won him the admiration of Nobunaga.

The remarkable alliance between these two so disparate men will last for more than twenty years. It is, of course, an alliance that serves both parties. For Ieyasu, it means the backing of a more powerful, and—at least then—more able tactician than himself. For Nobunaga, who by this time has turned his attention to the capital, it means a reliable defense in his rear, someone to guard Mikawa and Tōtōmi and face off a potential threat from powerful warlords towards the east: the Hōjō, the Uesugi, the Takeda.

Opposite page: Tokugawa Ieyasu in 1564, fighting Ikkō sectarians in Mikawa

The reality of such a threat is brought home in November 1572, when word reaches Hamamatsu Castle that Takeda Shingen has departed from

日本畧史圖
徳川家康公
内田正風記

Tokugawa Ieyasu's youth was a precarious one; more than once his life hung on a silk thread, but he seemed to have been born under a lucky star. At the age of three, he was separated from his mother. His father, Matsudaira Hirotada was the master of Okazaki Castle in the western part of Mikawa province, and a vassal to Imagawa Yoshimoto, the powerful warlord from the neighboring province of Suruga. Ieyasu's mother was from the Mizuno clan. But when Ieyasu was three years old, they allied themselves with the Oda, the arch-enemy of the Imagawa, forcing his father to divorce his wife and send her back to her clan.

Three years later, Takechiyo, as Ieyasu was then still called, was sent to Sunpu as a hostage to Imagawa Yoshimoto. He never arrived. On his way there his escort was intercepted by Oda men. He was packed off to Atsuta, the 41st station along the Tōkaidō, and put under the guardianship of Katō Yorimori, a vassal to Oda Nobunaga, the young master of Nagoya Castle, who controlled southern Owari. Yorimori's *yashiki* stood at a stone's throw from the ancient Atsuta Shrine. It is believed that, during his stay at Atsuta, Takechiyo first encountered the eccentric Nobunaga. And it is said that Nobunaga took a liking for the young boy, who was ten years his junior, often taking him along on his eccentric adventures.

For two years the life of the young boy hung in the balance, especially since his father refused to be blackmailed by the Oda. Then, in 1549, Takechiyo's father was assassinated by his own vassals. No longer of use to the Oda, the young boy was swapped in a hostage exchange with the Imagawa. Though technically a hostage of the Imagawa at Sunpu, given the death of his father, he now effectively became a member of the Imagawa clan. At Sunpu he became the pupil of the warrior-monk Tessai, who laid the solid foundation for the boy's stellar career. On his coming of age, he received part of Yoshimoto's name (Motonobu) and married the chieftain's niece and daughter of one of his vassals, Lady Tsukiyama. Nine years later, he fought his first battle, when he took part in the siege of Terabe Castle, whose master had defected to the Oda.

Ieyasu's alliance with Oda Nobunaga came at a high price. Being of Imagawa descent, Ieyasu's wife, Lady Tsukiyama, was far from happy with Ieyasu's alliance with Nobunaga, whom she held responsible for the demise of her clan—and with some justification. She especially took it out on Lady Tokuhime, the wife of her son, Nobuyasu, and the eldest daughter of that same Nobunaga, who failed to produce a legitimate heir to her precious son. Taking the matter in her own hands, she introduced several concubines into their household, all daughters of former Takeda vassals.

Refusing to accept this, Tokuhime wrote a long letter to her father, complaining of her mother-in-law's meddling in her marital affairs, accusing her of conducting an extramarital affair with her husband's Chinese physician, and—worst of all—implying he was a secret messenger in her attempts to get her son to form a pact against his father with the Takeda. Tokuhime's plan to take revenge on her mother-in-law backfired. Nobunaga was outraged and ordered his ally to kill his wife as well as his son. Not willing to jeopardize the alliance, Ieyasu complied, though he left it to his son to save face and commit ritual suicide.

Kōfu at the head of some twenty-five thousand troops and is marching down along the Tenryū River toward Hamamatsu. Ieyasu realises he and his clan are in grave danger. Shingen is formidable foe. From his power base of Kai province, he has steadily widened his sphere of influence to include large parts of Shinano, Kōzuke and Musashi. He is so confident that, unlike most warlords, he doesn't even have a castle, just a large mansion with a wide moat. This in accordance with his main motto: *hito wa shiro; hito wa ishigaki; hito wa hori* (men are castles; men are walls; men are moats)—in short, the shrewd warlord knew that it was all about human talent.

Any doubts that Shingen is aiming for Hamamatsu Castle are dispelled when, on 18 November, he lays siege to Futamata Castle, some ten miles north of Hamamatsu and Ieyasu's first line of defense. At the same time, he dispatches dozens of letters to Ieyasu's new vassals, promising them back their lands in return for their loyalty. He also sends out scouts to reconnoiter Tōtōmi and Mikawa and draw up detailed maps. At this point, Ieyasu's ally Nobunaga prudently advises him to retreat to Okazaki Castle in his home province of Mikawa and leave behind a skeleton force at Hamamatsu. But Ieyasu refuses. 'I'd rather break my sword and become a monk that surrender all that I have gained at the first threat of danger.' He decides to stay put

Ieyasu (right) hears of Shingen's approach

Opposite page: Takeda Shingen

at Hamamatsu Castle, though the odds are firmly against him. With a third of his men spread over his growing territory, he is left with only eight thousand men. Tied down in his own battles, Nobunaga can't come to his ally's help, though he does promise reinforcements.

For two anxious months, Ieyasu waits for Nobunaga's troops to arrive. All the while he is being harried by messengers from Futamata Castle, imploring him to come to their aid. Painfully aware that he has too few men to come to their aid, he decides to stay put. Finally, towards the middle of January, Nobunaga's reinforcements arrive. But relief turns to disappointment when Ieyasu realizes they're only three thousand men strong. Even with Nobunaga's reinforcements, he is still outnumbered by more than two to one. And they're too late. A few days later, on January 22, 1573, having put

Old map of Tōtōmi, split through the center by the Tenryū River

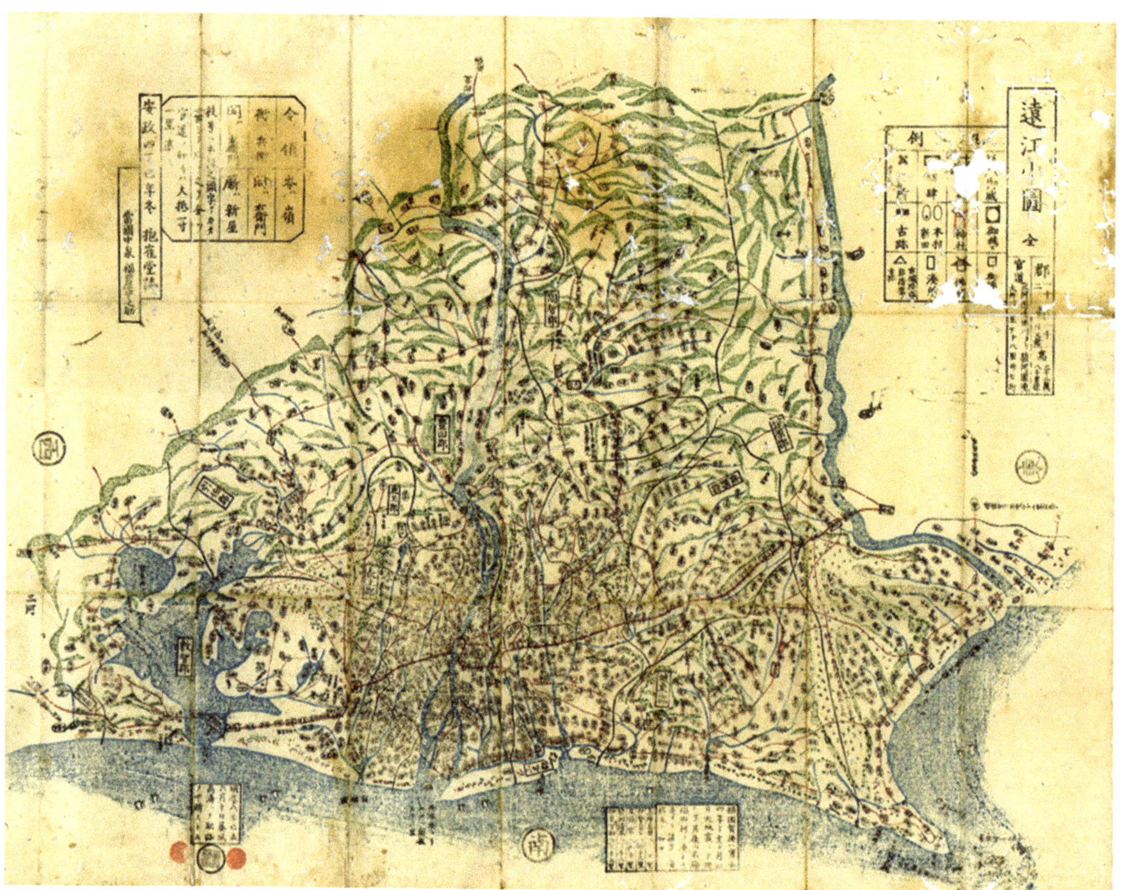

月百姿

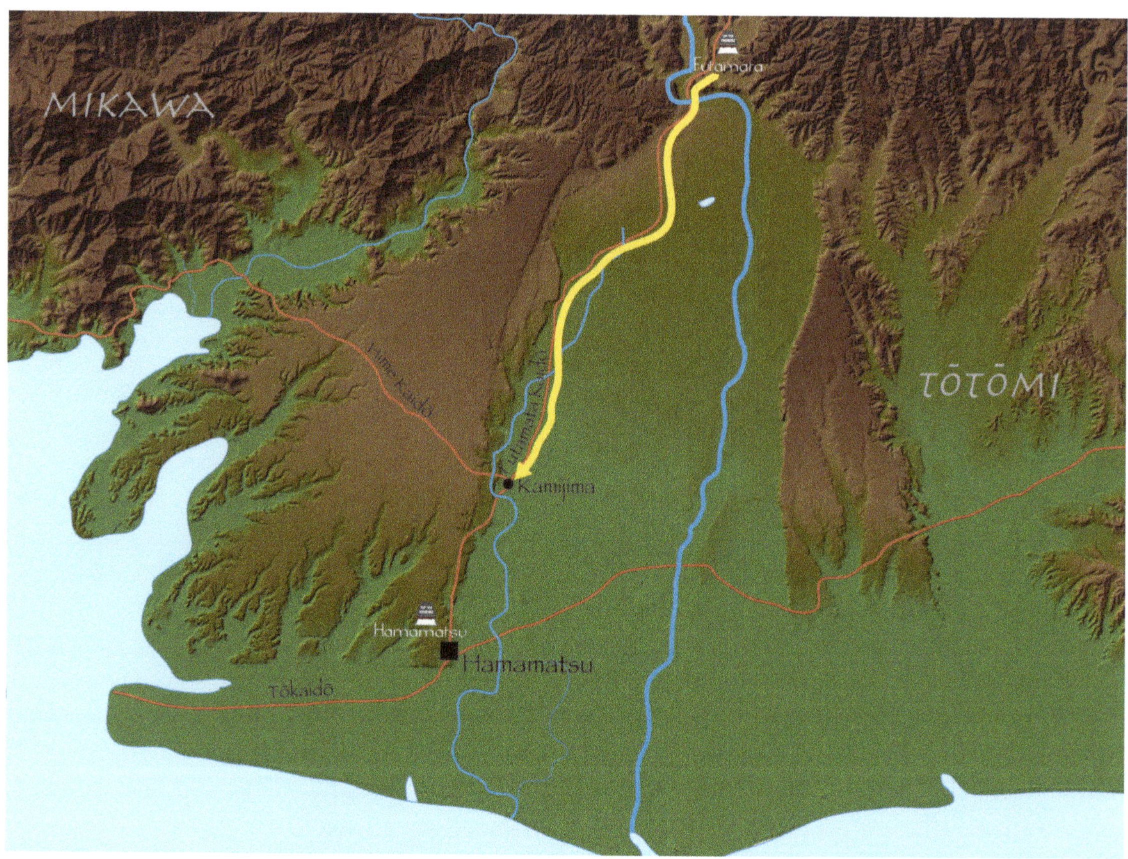

up a stiff fight, but with their water supply cut off, Ieyasu's men at Futamata are finally forced to surrender to Shingen.

Two days later, Ieyasu's scouts tell him that Shingen is on the move again. He is following the Futamata Highroad and is heading straight for Hamamatsu. Ieyasu convenes a war council with his retainers and Nobunaga's generals. All of them favor a defensive strategy; to prepare for a siege and hold the castle. Hamamatsu Castle is one of the strongest in the region, so it shouldn't be a hard thing to do. But Ieyasu thinks otherwise. The *Mikawa monogatari* describes how he angrily retorted:

> What kind of reasoning is that? Who would stand by and let a large force pass by the back entrance of one's *yashiki* and remain inside with-

> out rushing out and challenging them? Isn't it natural to challenge them, even if one were to be defeated? Likewise, how can we not challenge someone trespassing on our domain, even if their's is a large army? At least we should go out and fight! Battles aren't decided by numbers; they're decided by higher powers.

Though spoken with passion, they are words that will soon come to haunt him. By the morning of January 25, Shingen's forces are within a few miles of Hamamatsu. It seems they are about to lay siege of the castle. But then something strange happens. Having reached the hamlet of Kamijima, his forces suddenly turn and head west, up the Hime Highroad towards Kiga. Soon they are on Mikatagahara, an elevated plain just north of Hamamatsu.

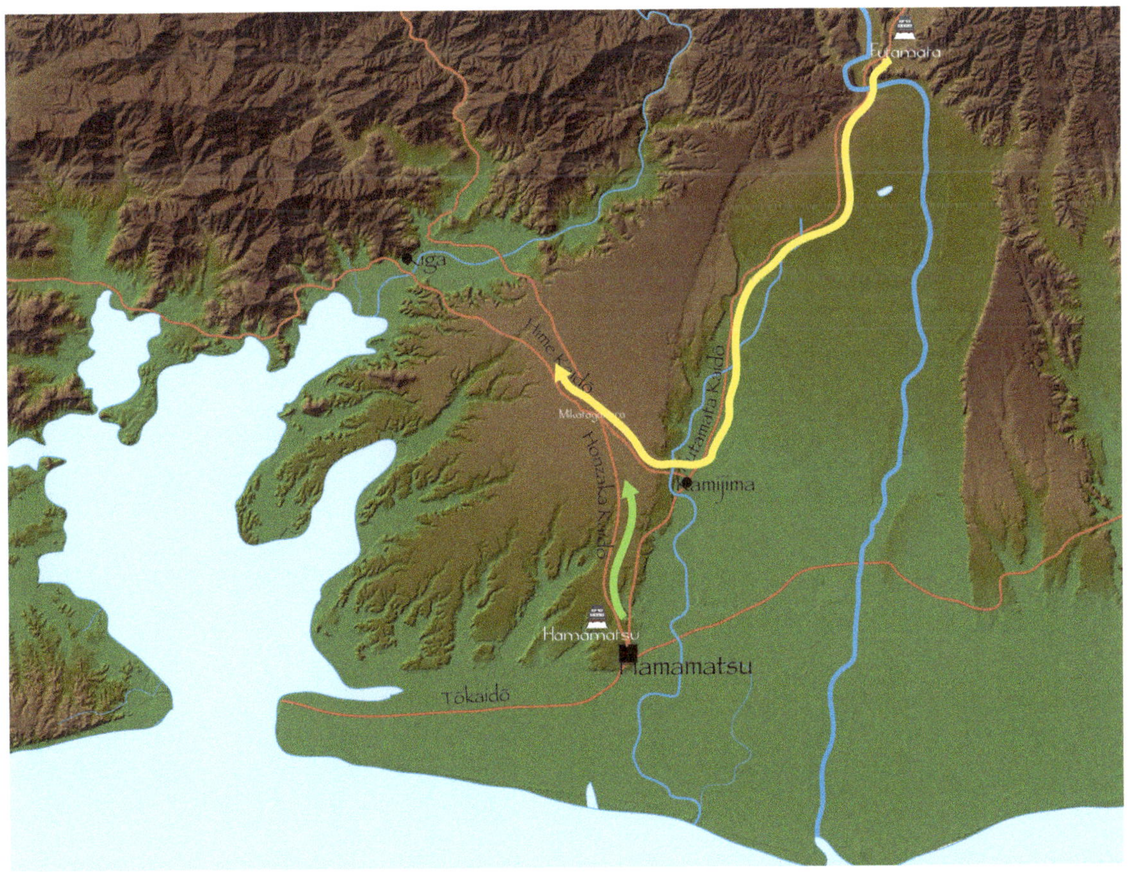

Ieyasu is stunned: can it be that Shingen is turning his back on him? This is the chance he has been waiting for. Though the plain is wide and flat, the road leading down the other side is steep and narrow; if he can attach Shingen in the rear there he will have him trapped.

Rallying his troops, Ieyasu hastily sets out along the Honzaka Highroad, which intersects the Hime Highroad at the center of Mikatagahara. He reckons that by the time he catches up with his enemy, Shingen's troops will just about have started their steep descent on the plain's opposite side. But no sooner has he reached the plateau than his blood runs cold. There, facing him in full glory, is the combined force of Shingen's army in full battle array. Arranged in the impenetrable Fish Scale formation, their black banners boldly proclaim the Takeda battle cry: *fūrinkazan* (swift as the wind; quiet as a forest; fierce as fire; immovable like a mountain).

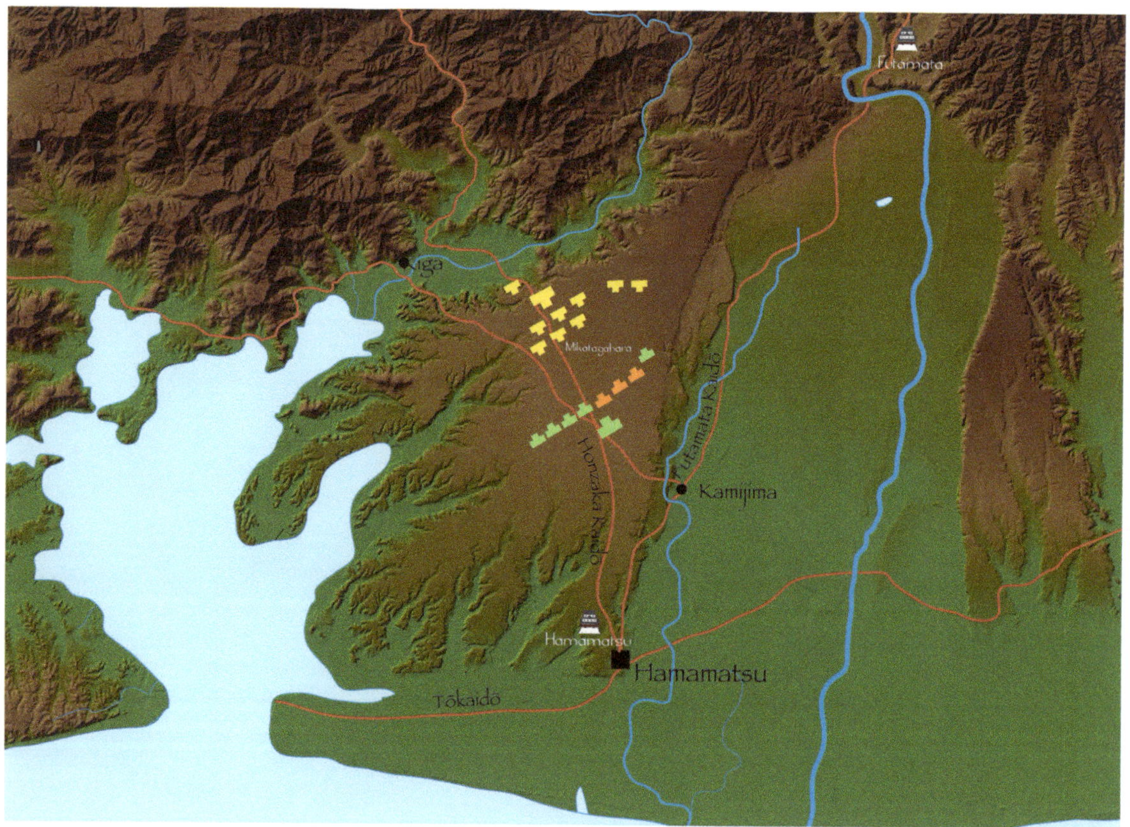

Naitō Masashige (center) and Honda Tadakatsu (right) engage the enemy

Ieyasu has made the biggest blunder of his career, and he knows it. The wily fox has lured him from his castle. Now he is the one who is trapped, for there is no way he can descend the plain without falling in the very same trap he had intended for his foe. Hastily he orders his troops into the Crane Wing battle array. On his left are his Mikawa warriors under four of his vassals. On his right are Nobunaga's reinforcements under the command of three of Nobunaga's generals, flanked by more Mikawa men under Sakai Tadatsugu. Again, Ieyasu is advised not to attack the enemy head-on but to let Shingen take the initiative and try to hit him in the flank or rear. But again Ieyasu brushes aside their concerns and orders a frontal assault on Shingen's vanguard.

Shingen's vanguard of three thousand *ashigaru* responds in kind. Armed with slingshots and stones, they attack Ieyasu's righthand flank. Breaching the gaps that have fallen, they raise the Takeda battle cry and fall on the Nobunaga reinforcements. Then, as if stung by a hornet, the whole of Shingen's army begins to move forward. Before long they clash with the rest of Ieyasu's army, and soon the whole front is engaged in battle. It is mainly due

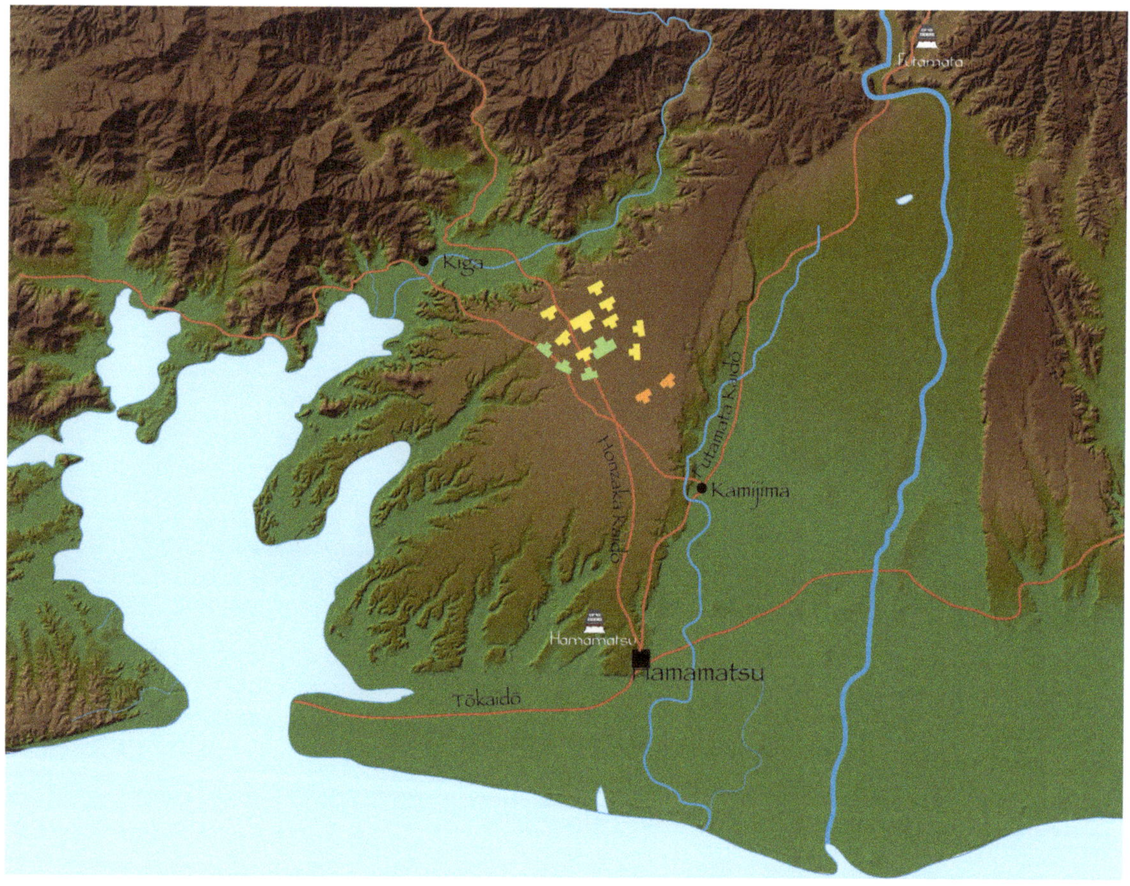

to the fierce assault of Ieyasu's Mikawa warriors that the Takeda advance is halted and even forced to retreat by several hundred yards. Shingen's vanguard, however, keeps on pressing home and before long the Nobunaga reinforcements, who have less heart for a fight, begin to give way, leaving Sakai Tadatsugu in the lurch. The latter refuses to give ground, and with superhuman effort finally brings Shingen's vanguard to a halt.

Sensing his vanguard's fatigue, Shingen now throws fresh troops into the battle. Again Tadatsugu and his men throw themselves headlong on their enemy. But just then Shingen's son, Katsuyori, launches a withering attack on Ieyasu's front. This blithering new assault is just too much for Ieyasu's men. Tadatsugu's men are wiped out. Only one of Nobunaga's commanders stands his ground but soon pays for his valiance with his life. So do many of the Mikawa men, especially those who are eager to redeem themselves for letting Futamata Castle fall into enemy hands. Ieyasu, too, grabs a lance and throws himself into the battle with his guard, penetrating far into enemy lines. But it is not enough; Shingen's army, by now honed to perfection in countless battles, shakes this off too; its Fish Scale formation remains impenetrable. Only a barrage of rifle fire seems to make a dent. Shingen meanwhile orders more troops to join the battle; up to three rows deep and responsive to Shingen's each and every command, his cavalry obliterate what is left of Ieyasu's army and is about to trample his standard, which is placed slightly to the rear.

Ieyasu is overcome by grief over his terrible mistake. Realizing his game is up, he unsheathes his longsword with his right hand and takes the reins of his horse in his left: he is ready to fight to the death. Seeing this, Natsume Yoshinobu, who had remained behind as captain of the garrison of Hamamatsu Castle, but has rushed to Ieyasu's aid with two dozen guards, grabs the reins of Ieyasu's horse and calls out, "Why sacrifice yourself? let me fall in your place!" Saying this, he turns around Ieyasu's horse and brings the haft of his lance down on its rump. Startled, the horse bolts, carrying Ieyasu toward his castle and safety. Several times, Shingen's men attempt to thwart

Natsume Yoshinobu (mouth agape) offers up his life for his lord

Ieyasu (right) makes his escape

Ieyasu's retreat, but one is kicked down by Ieyasu's guard, another struck down by one of Ieyasu's arrows.

Safely back at his castle, Ieyasu immediately orders his men to leave the front gate wide open and light huge fires. At the same time, he orders Tadatsugu—who has miraculously also made it back alive—to have his men beat huge *taikō* drums to guide the others home.

The *Mikawa monogatari* describes how at this low point, one of Ieyasu's retainers, a warrior by the name of Ōkubo Tadayo, turns to his master and says:

> 'By staying here inside the castle we will surely embolden the enemy even more. Let me take all our remaining musketeers and launch a night attack against the enemy encampment!'

And so it happens. That same night, Tadayo and his men attack Shingen and his warriors, who have set up camp for the night at Saigake, just a mile north from Hamamatsu Castle. It is just a pinprick, but it is enough to tip the psychological balance in Ieyasu's favor. Though fierce warriors, Shingen's generals become wary: the fires at the castle, the commotion, combined with this unexpected night attack, all causes them to believe Ieyasu is setting a trap. They advise their lord not to attack the castle. Shingen isn't that convinced, yet he always heeds the counsel of his men, and that same night he decides to withdraw.

In the end, Ieyasu is only saved by the late hour at which the battle has commenced and the valiance of his men; not his own skill. Nobunaga, who had foreseen the outcome of such an uneven fight—both in sheer numbers and the experience of its commander—comments on Ieyasu's defeat with the words: '*Furyō no ni teitaraku sōrō*' ('His impudence has landed him quite a mess!'). Coming from Nobunaga, it is only a mild reproach. At the same time, Nobunaga expels from his service his general, Sakuma Nobumori, for saving his now skin at the cost of his fellow commanders.

Ieyasu now does a remarkable thing. He orders an artist to Hamamatsu Castle and has him paint his portrait. The result is far from flattering, for Ieyasu, who is said to have vacated his bowels at one point in the heat of battle, is clearly still rattled by his brush with death—it is all there: the terror of facing death, the shame of defeat, the anguish of what lies ahead. It is said

Sakai Tadatsugu beats the *taikō* to guide the men home

Ieyasu's haunting portrait, painted in the wake of the battle

that much later, after he had pacified the country, purveying his realm from his new capital of Edo, Ieyasu still reserved a place in his quarters on the grounds of Edo Castle for this haunting painting, as if to remind himself of how close he had come by not heeding his own better instincts and the good counsel of his allies.

NAGASHINO

In the spring of 1573, four months after he has humiliated Ieyasu at Mikatagahara, Takeda Shingen, one of the great warlords of the Warring States Period is dead. Already in the wake of that battle, as he is inspecting the severed heads of his slain enemies at Saigake, a sudden, recurring lung hemorrhage causes him to vomit up blood. It has forced him to withdraw to Nagashino Castle for several months of rest. But on the thirteenth of May, while withdrawing his troops to Kōfu, the hemorrhage suddenly returns and he dies along the roadside. With his death, the Oda-Tokugawa alliance is temporarily relieved of a dangerous enemy, that threatens their drive towards unification. But it is only that: a temporary relief. The Takeda clan and its fearsome cavalry are still intact. At its head now stands Takeda Katsuyori, a man who—if not as shrewd as his father—at least equals him in his love of a good fight.

It isn't just his martial spirit that drives the young Katsuyori to prove himself in battle. The son of a mere concubine, Katsuyori has always felt a sense of insecurity—a sense only amplified by the immense martial stature of his father. After all, it is only the premature death of Shingen's eldest son and heir, Yoshinobu, that has propelled Katsuyori to the forefront. Had it not been for Yoshinobu's attempt to overthrow his father, Katsuyori would never have been at the helm of the Takeda clan. Shingen's will, drafted while encamped along the Mikawa Highway as his condition gradually worsened, also leaves little doubt about Katsuyori's prospects within the Takeda clan. Not being of the same blood, Katsuyori is not allowed to use in his name the character for 'Nobu' like his brothers. Nor is he allowed to carry into battle banners with the famous Takeda motto, *fūrinkazan* (swift as the wind; quiet as a forest; fierce as fire; immovable like a mountain). Perhaps most hurtful to Katsuyori's sense of pride is Shingen's injunction to keep his death a closely guarded secret for the next three years. Even after that, Katsuyori isn't to assume real clan leadership, but to act as a guardian to his own seven-year-old son, Nobukatsu, until he has come of age.

Reason enough, then, for Katsuyori to prove his mettle. The first time he seriously does so is in the summer of 1574 when he captures from Ieyasu Takatenjin Castle in eastern Tōtōmi, a feat his father has often tried but failed to accomplish. Emboldened by his success, Katsuyori now turns his attention toward Nagashino Castle in Mikawa, which Ieyasu has recaptured from the

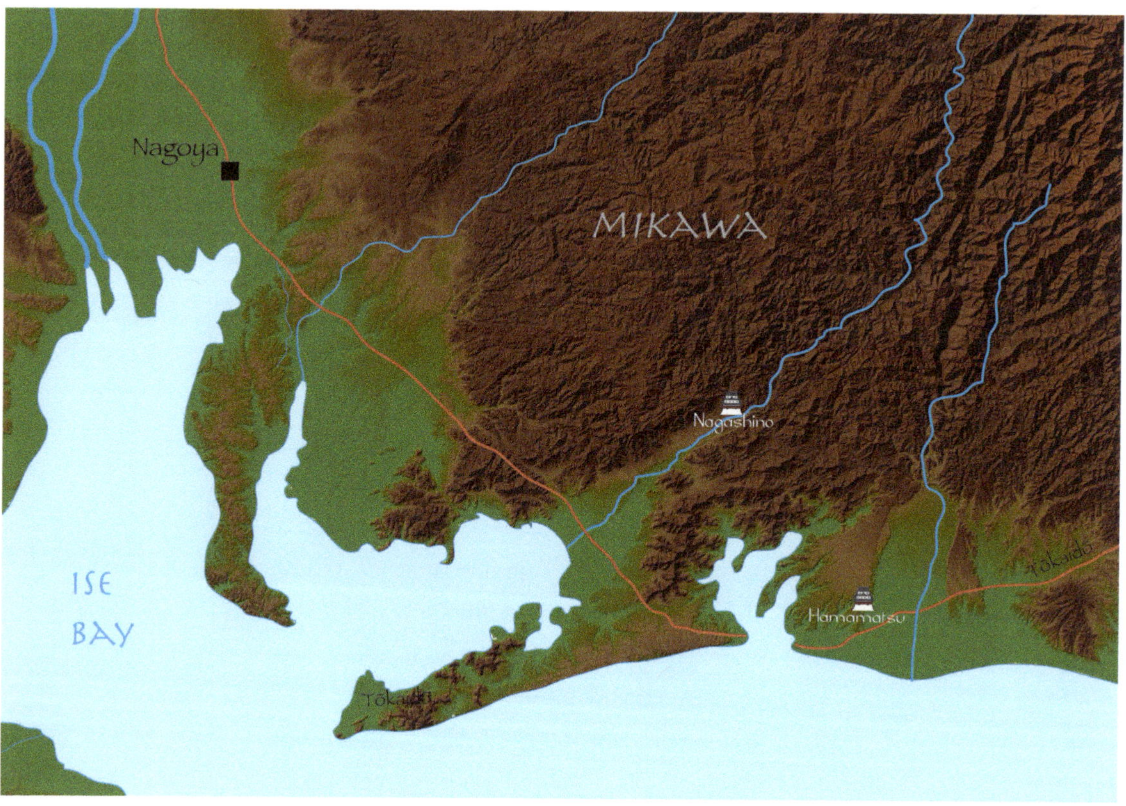

Takeda Shingen was the most formidable of all Nobunaga's many enemies. Much has been made of his prowess as a military commander on the battlefield. Over many years of honing his men, he made his cavalry the most feared among warriors. Yet to Shingen doing battle was just one aspect of warfare; diplomacy, politics, economics, and even religeon were equally important tools to achieve his aims.

His main aim was to add more territory to his domain, not so much to satisfy his own ambitions, but to keep in check his retainers, for Kai's chieftains were fiercely independent in spirit. Even his father, Nobutora, who restored his clan's rule over Kai province after decades of unrest, was only able to do so by giving his retainers great sway in his clan counsels. Shingen's way of keeping them together was by conquering more territory, which he then distributes among them.

By the end of the 1560s Shingen had conquered much of Shinano, Kōzuke and Musashi. He was so confident of his power that he didn't reside in a castle, just a large mansion with a wide moat. This in accordance with his main motto: *hito wa shiro; hito wa ishigaki; hito wa hori* (men are castles; men are walls; men are moats)—men, specifically his retainers, were his most important asset. And it is here that Shingen differed profoundly from Nobunaga, for the latter realized that to achieve his objective of centralized control he had to wean his vassals from their lands. And where Nobunaga took one step after another to separate chieftains from their lands, Shingen spent his career handing out territory to his vassals.

Much of that territory lay in the neighboring province of Shinano, which lay to the northwest of Shingen's home province of Kai and had no real strongman. To cover his rear he had formed alliances with the Imagawa and the Hōjō. And it was through his northwestern expansion into Shinano that Shingen came into conflict with his most famed rival: Uesugi Kenshin, the warlord of Echigo, which bordered on Shinano from the north.

It is believed the two rivals met in battle at Kawanakajima as many as five times. The fiercest encounter was in 1561, when some 40.000 men locked in combat. Both leaders claimed victory, but in truth it made neither of them any the wiser. Their battles had no lasting effect on the distribution of power in the country as a whole, as they were fought on the periphery of the medieval centers of power, the Kantō and the Kinai regions.

The former site of Nagashino Castle

Takeda following Shingen's death. The castle stands on the front line between the Takeda and Tokugawa territories, forming the Oda-Tokugawa alliance's first line of defense against the Takeda's westwards ambitions. In the spring of 1575, he marched into Mikawa at the head of an army of fifteen thousand men and, on 16 June, lays siege to Nagashino Castle.

Back at his headquarters of Okazaki Castle, Ieyasu refuses to budge. His defeat at Mikatagahara has taught him an important lesson: not to make rash decisions. All his hopes are now pinned on Nagashino Castle. Sitting on the tip of a small peninsula in the confluence of the Samusa and Ure Rivers, it has great natural defenses. The earthen walls around the inner citadel have been raised, and on the northern side, where the castle is most vulnerable to attack, a third moat has been added to the existing two. Yet the castle's garrison of five hundred men are armed with just two-hundred muskets, but against Katsuyori's fifteen thousand their odds are slim.

Within days of his arrival, Katsuyori makes his first attempt to breach the castle's defenses. It is now the rainy season and launching rafts across the wide Ure River he tries to mine the castle, but his men are thrown back and many of the rafts are overturned in the raging river. More assaults follow and for several days the castle's defenders resist the fierce attacks. But on the third day, an incendiary arrow sets fire to the castle's granary, causing most of their provisions to be lost in the flames. Its defenders now have only a few days left before they will run out of food.

At this critical stage in the castle's defense, the castle's master, Okudaira Nobumasa, decides to send a messenger to Okazaki Castle to ask Ieyasu for reinforcements. Torii Suneemon, manages to smuggle himself through the Takeda cordon and safely reach Okazaki Castle. There he is told that help is at hand. Oda Nobunaga has raised a force of thirty thousand warriors, while Ieyasu himself stands ready to march with another eight. Hurrying back, Suneemon reaches the vicinity of the castle on 24 June. Lighting a signal fire at the crest of a nearby mountain to alert those inside the castle of his arrival, he seeks to slip through the Takeda cordon. But this time he is caught

Torii Suneemon breaks through the Takeda cordon

The *Mikawa monogatari* describes how Suneemon is led before Katsuyori, who, hearing of Suneemon's mission, makes him a proposition:

> 'I will spare your life. Indeed, I will let you live in my province and bestow on you your own lands. But first I will tie you to a cross and erect it in front of the castle for all to see. And you will then call out to them and say, "Lord Nobunaga will not come to your rescue. You had better surrender the castle." After that, we will untie you again and let you go.'

Suneemon consents and lets himself be tied to the cross and be placed in front of Nagashino Castle. Then, at the top of his voice, he bellows:

> 'The Takeda have promised me my life, as well as lands if I say Lord Nobunaga will not march. However, already Lord Nobunaga has said he shall march from Okazaki. Likewise, Lord Ieyasu and his son, master Nobuyasu, have marched towards Nodawara. Hold out and keep the castle! Within a few days, your fortunes will reverse!'

Suneemon (center) encourages those inside the castle to hold out in front of Katsuyori (on horseback)

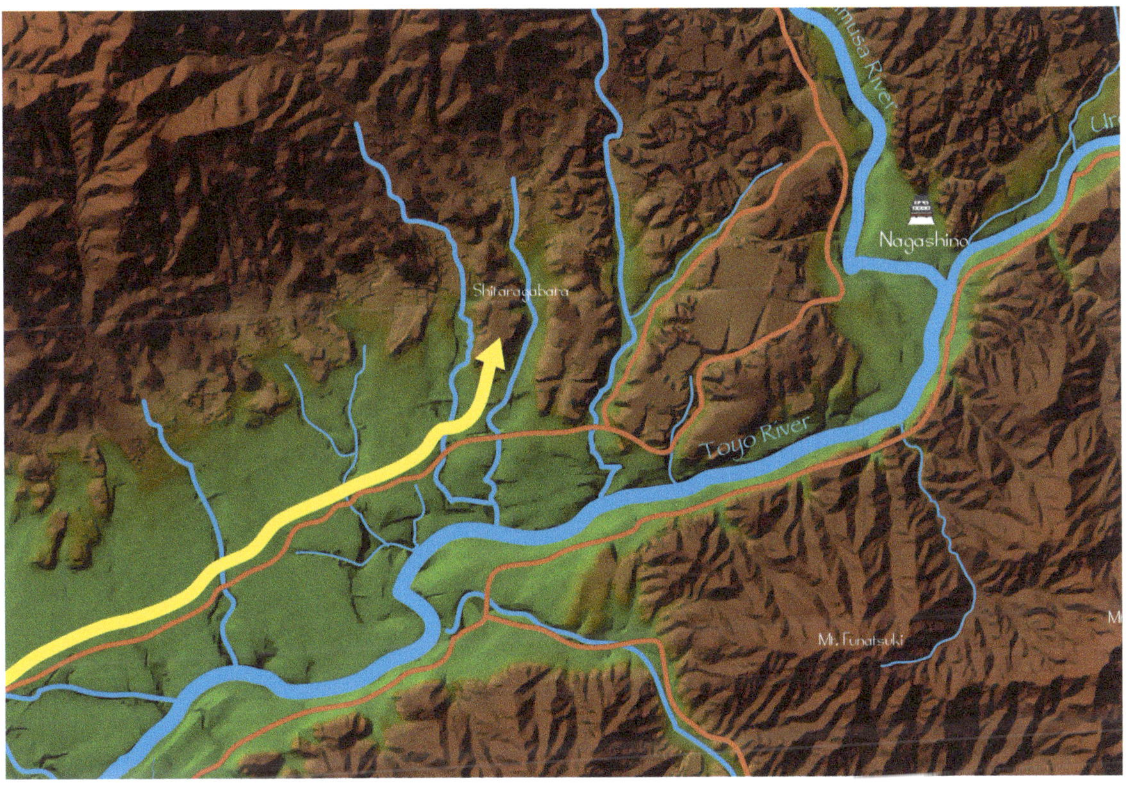

They are Suneemon's last words; enraged by the messenger's ploy Katsuyori orders his men to spear him on the cross.

But those inside the castle hold out, and two days later, on 26 June, the huge Oda-Tokugawa juggernaut reaches Nagashino and sets up camp at Shitaragabara, a slightly elevated hill along the Rengo River, some two miles west of Nagashino Castle as the crow flies. It has taken Nobunaga's army five long days to get there. He has spent one night at Atsuta (where he takes time to inspect the famous shrine and orders his head carpenter to draw up plans for its restoration), two at Ieyasu's headquarters of Okazaki Castle, one night at Ushikubo Castle, and one night at Nodawara, even though it is just four miles downstream from Shitaragabara. It leaves Katsyori with the distinct impression his enemy is stalling, keen to avoid a fight.

But Nobunaga has slowed down on purpose; he wants Katsuyori to feel overly confident. He also wants to draw him away from Nagashino Castle;

to a place where he himself will be in control of the battlefield. And Shitaragabara is just the right place. Overlooking the Toyo River delta from the west, the elongated hill is pincered between two tributaries of the Toyo River, thus forming natural moats. But this is not yet enough for Nobunaga. Over the next two days, using the cover of the driving rain, he sets his men to turn the hill into a so-called *jinjiro*—a makeshift bastion—leveling the tops by cutting down the densely growing trees. Its slopes, too, are reshaped, turning them into steep and staggered parapets. At the foot of these, the lumbered wood is used to erect thick stockades behind dry moats that stretch the length of the hill. Behind these stockades, he positions some three thousand marksmen, armed with muskets and bows and arrows. To make them as effective as possible he orders them to hold their fire as long as possible, right up until the moment the enemy will be close up to the stockades. Over the previous months, they have been drilled in the Western art of volley fire. It is a totally new concept of warfare that requires a high degree of discipline among the musketeers.

Learning that Nobunaga and Ieyasu have finally arrived, Katsuyori convenes a war council. Old Takeda hands, who have served under his father and are used to having their voices heard, advise the young chieftain to withdraw or at least put all his efforts in taking the castle so that they will have an advantage there. But the headstrong Katsuyori, intent on having his own way, ignores them. The next day, June 28, leaving three thousand men behind, he divides the rest of his force into three units that take up positions on a ridge just east of Shitaragabara.

Katsuyori does not share his generals' misgivings. Far from it. Writing to one of his chieftains back home that same day, the young commander seems supremely confident in the superiority of the Takeda cavalry and the inevitable outcome of the pending battle:

To Miura Samanosuke,

I was very grateful for you going out of your way to send me a messenger to express your concerns about our position here at Nagashino. Yet everything is going exactly to plan, so you needn't worry. It is true

Opposite page: A young and overly confident Takeda Katsuyori

武田勝頼
一猛齋芳虎画

that, since I've surrounded Ieyasu's castle of Nagashino, he and Nobunaga have sent reinforcement in an attempt to attack me from the rear, but it is nothing serious and our armies are now facing each other on the field of battle. Indeed, Ieyasu and Nobunaga seem so intimidated and at a loss what to do that I will attack their camp in one charge and crush them with ease.

Katsuyori

Convening a war council of his own that evening, Nobunaga is in equally good spirits. And with good reason. His plan to draw his opponent into a position of disadvantage has worked, and he observes, 'him taking up position there is a godsend; we will claim victory without the loss of a single man.' Sakai Tadatsugu, Ieyasu's general who played such a crucial role in the Battle of Mikatagahara, suggests taking a detachment to simultaneously launch a surprise attack on the Takeda warriors still encamped near Nagashino Castle. Nobunaga dismisses it: 'For a country warrior like you it might seem a good plan, but this is not the way we do battle.' But afterward, when it has grown dark, he calls Tadatsugu to his tent and commends him for his plan. He puts him in command of some two thousand marksmen,

The two armies face each other across the Rengo River, while Sakai and his men (right) releive those withing the castle

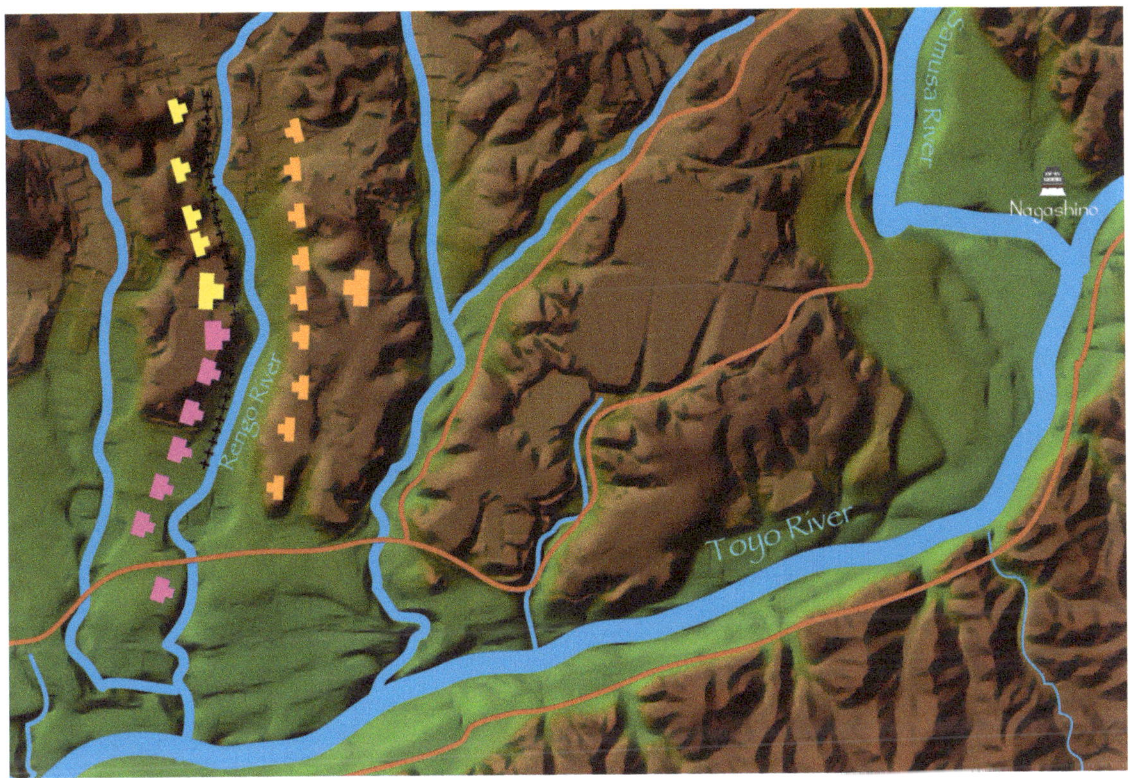

though he urges him to slip away under the cover of night—it is another example of Nobunaga playing his cards close to his chest.

Early next morning, June 29, at the hour of the Rabbit, rifle fire can be heard from the direction of Nagashino Castle: Sakai and his men have launched their surprise attack. Breaking through the cordon, they unite with those within the castle and together launch a counterattack, setting fire to their camp. Utterly surprised, the Takeda warriors turn and flee northwards in the direction of the Hōrai Temple on the slopes of Mount Hōraiji.

It is just over a mile as the crow flies from the castle to where Ieyasu and Nobunaga are encamped and the shots can be clearly heard. The *Shinchō kōki* describes how:

> Going over to Ieyasu's camp, Nobunaga climbed Takamatsu-*yama*, a shallow hill just behind Ieyasu's camp, from where he began to issue

The Takeda cavalry is wiped out by Nobunaga's musketeers

orders, making adjustments in time to make sure his troops move accordingly. Then he ordered some one-hundred musketeers forward, and arranging them in groups under the command of *teppō bugyō* Sasa Masamori, Maeda Matasaemon Toshiie, Nonomura Sanjūrō, Fukutomi Tairasaemon Hidekatsu, and Ban Kyūsaburō Naomasa, sent them outside the stockade to take potshots at the Takeda *ashigaru*.

Again Katsuyori reacts predictably. He orders one of his chief generals, Yamagata Masakage, to launch a frontal assault on the left flank of the enemy positions. Spurred on by men beating large *taikō* drums, they rush across the narrow valley. But well before they reach the stockade they are mowed down by a barrage of musket fire. For the first time in Japanese martial history, the devastating effect of volley fire is felt on the battlefield. Rotating in close succession, Nobunaga's musketeers unload a hail of molten lead on the Takeda utterly devastating in its deadly effectiveness. A second assault from the Takeda center under the command of Katsuyori's uncle, Nobukado, who like Masakage, has been one of Shingen's twenty-four generals, goes about it more systematically, rotating his men as they seek to tackle their enemy's defenses. But when half of them too are killed, he orders the remainder to retreat. A third and fourth assault achieves just as little, apart from helping to pile up the corpses of men and horses so high that they begin to form a barrier in themselves. At length, aware the battle is lost, Katsuyori orders his men to withdraw, leaving behind some ten thousand fellow warriors.

Nobunaga's prediction that they would not lose a single man may have been overly optimistic, but given his disregard of the individual, he may have meant 'a single commander.' And in this he has been right. Not so Katsuyori; he leaves behind ten of his bravest and most experienced commanders. Among them is Baba Nobuharu, whose bravery in spite of the odds is so outstanding that even Nobunaga's chroniclers, who usually exert themselves in merely praising their lord's eternal wisdom and unending courage, feel compelled to comment on Nobuharu's brave example.

Baba Nobuharu sets a valiant example

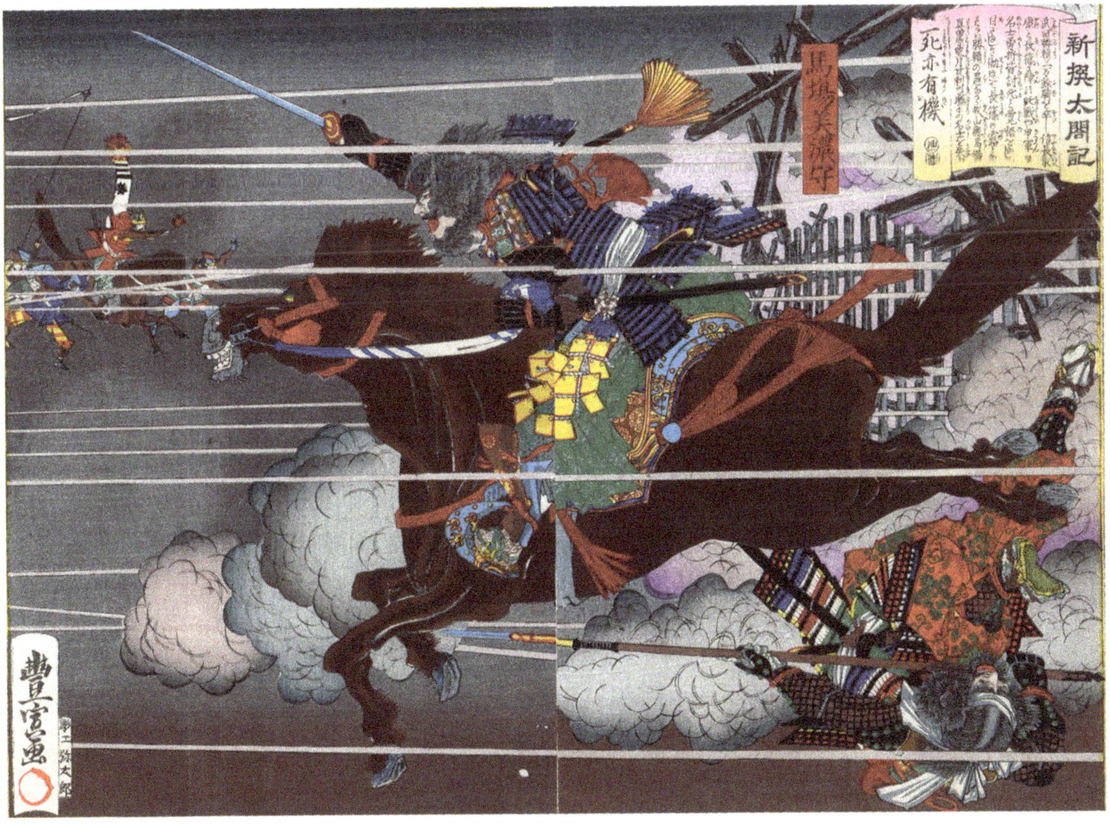

The ***Kōyō gunkan*** was originally conceived by Kasuga Toratsuna, alias Kōsaka Masanobu (right), one of Shingen's Four Heavenly Kings (Shitennō), or chief retainers. Starting in early 1575, Toratsuna began to dictate its first draft to his nephew, Kasuga Sōjirō, as he grew increasingly worried about the future of Takeda clan under Shingen's son. Within months after he had started his life's work, Toratsuna saw his worst fears confirmed when Katsuyori suffered a crushing defeat at Nagashino. More motivated than ever to record his recollections for posterity, Toratsuna spent much of the next two years dictating to his nephew all he knew about his former lord and master Shingen, about his son Katsuyori, about the Takeda clan as a whole, and its art of warfare.

Following Toratsuna's death, in 1578, his nephew, Sōjirō, from his refuge on the Island of Sadoshima, continued to follow and chronicle the demise and tragic end of the clan he and his uncle had served for so long, until he too passed away, in 1585.

Following Sōjirō's death, the multiple-volume work fell into the hands of Obata Mitsumori, another former Takeda vassal. He had been garrison commander of the second tier of Kaizu Castle, but had meanwhile entered the service of Uesugi Kagekatsu as an *ashigaru taishō*. From Mitsumori, the work was passed on within the Obata clan until, towards the end of the sixteenth century, it came into the possession of Obata Kagenori. And it was under Kagenori's editorship that the *Kōyō gunkan* evolved into its final twenty-volume edition.

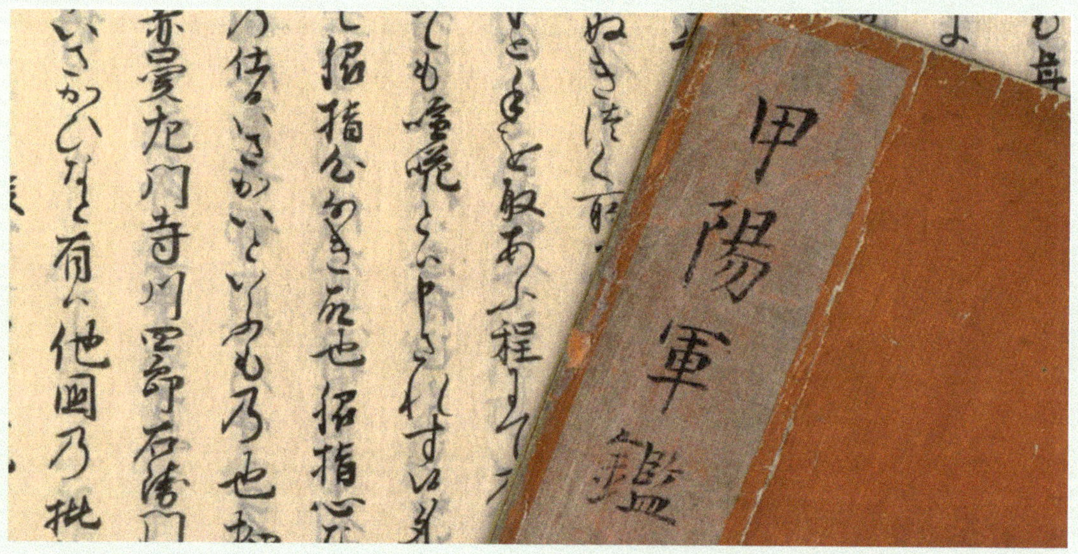

Katsuyori and his followers are hunted down

Eight more years Katsuyori manages to cling on to what remains, though—largely through his own fault—it grows less and less. In the end, he is hunted down to the foot of Mount Tenmoku with his last loyal retainers, among them a man by the name of Tsuchiya Sukerokurō. The *Kōyō gunkan* describes how:

> At length, having exhausted all his arrows, master Tsuchiya was about to draw his sword when he was struck by six enemy *yari* at once. Rushing to his side, Lord Katsuyori parried the yari and singlehandedly struck down the six enemy warriors. Yet three more warriors struck out with their *yari*, one piercing his throat, the two others his lower side, and pinning down Lord Katsuyori to the ground, they took his lordship's head.

When Katsuyori's severed head is finally presented to Nobunaga for inspection, the latter scolds it saying, "It was your father wanted to march on the capital, but instead it is your head that will be on display there.' Not so Ieyasu, who has Katsuyori's head placed on a dais and laments the warrior's

Katsuyori and his family meet their end at the foot of Mount Tenmoku

youthful impetuosity in not heeding the counsel of his generals. In doing so he may have cast his mind back only two years when like Katsuyori, he too failed to heed the advice of his men and rushed headlong into the trap set so skillfully by Katsuyori's father. He too had lost many good men, and it had only been through their bravery that his life had been saved. Katsuyori's men had offered themselves so he might have another chance to restore the Takeda fortunes. But instead of learning from his mistakes he had added new ones until finally, he had run out of luck as well as good men.

But the Takeda legacy lives on. Not only in the annals of history, but also on the battlefield. Following the demise of the Takeda clan, Ieyasu hires many of their warriors. Among them is a certain Obata Kagenori, the man who has spent the better part of his life compiling the *Kōyō gunkan*, the revolutionary work on the Takeda clan's unparalleled mastery of battlefield tactics. Adding Kai to his territory following Nobunaga's death, he orders a temple, the Keitoku-in, to be built along the Kōshū Kaidō, for the repose of Katsuyori's soul and those of his family.

HONŌ-JI

It is the summer of 1582. Oda Nobunaga is at the height of his powers. He has subdued many of his rivals in a brilliant campaign that began with his stunning victory over Imagawa Yoshimoto with an army six times smaller than his enemy. He has also been lucky; two of his most dangerous rivals, Takeda Shingen and Uesugi Kenshin have both died natural deaths. And their clans have been neutralized: the Uesugi through internal rivalry; the Takada through Nobunaga and Ieyasu's crushing victory at Nagashino over Shingen's son, Katsuyori. Japan's major sects, too, have been eviscerated, first at Hieizan, then at Nagashima, and finally at Ishiyama, after ten years of campaigning in which no quarter is given.

Yet Nobunaga's life's work—to unify the country—is nowhere near complete. Through subjugation, persuasion, and marriage he has forged numerous alliances, yet large parts of Japan are still controlled by warlords less inclined to follow suit, the Hōjō in the Kantō (though they do pay tribute), the Chōsokabe in the island of Shikoku (though Nobunaga has only recently conducted the coming-of-age ceremony (*genpuku*) for the son of chieftain Chōsokabe Motochika). Yet it is especially the powerful Mōri who preoccupy Nobunaga at this stage in his campaign. Safely ensconced in their powerful citadel of Takamatsu Castle, they fiercely resist all attempts to constrain their drive towards expansion in the west.

In this drive to modernization, Nobunaga relies very much on his alliance with Tokugawa Ieyasu. For more than two decades now the two warlords have worked closely together. It is a utilitarian alliance, built on the mutual benefits to both men, but also on a shared vision for a unified Japan. He also relies heavily on two of his generals: Hashiba (Toyotomi) Hideyoshi and Akechi Mitsuhide. Of these two Hideyoshi is perhaps the more brilliant general. Having started out as a commander of a unit of *ashigaru* (foot soldiers), Hideyoshi already is present in many of Nobunaga's early campaigns, many of them against castles under the control of the rivaling Saitō clan in Ōmi. It is during this time that his signature of Kinoshita Hideyoshi first appears in some of the formal records of the Oda clan—a clear sign that he is now a recognized commander in Nobunaga's military.

Hideyoshi enters Nobunaga's service

Toyotomi Hideyoshi was of such obscure origins that we're not even sure when exactly he was born, nor what his exact background was. The *Taikō sosei-ki* claims he was born to Konoshita Yaemon, an *ashigaru* (foot soldier) who lived in the village of Nakamura, which lay at a stone's throw from Oda Nobunaga's birthplace of Shobata Castle. This would automatically have made his father someone who was in the service of the Oda clan. Other sources claim his parents were peasants, or even entertainers, hired to amuse Nobunaga at his castle. Whatever his background, it can't have been too impressive, for Hideyoshi himself forbade historians to mention his actual descent, as it interfered with his somewhat self-insecure claim of being of imperial descent.

What is certain is that, somewhere in the 1540s, he entered the service of Matsushita Yukitsuna, the master of Zudaji Castle in Tōtōmi, and a vassal of the then still powerful Imagawa. He didn't stay in his service for long, for only a few years later, in 1554, he returned home and entered the service of Oda Nobunaga as an errand boy. The *Taikō-ki* claims that, on his way home, while resting his weary body against a pillar of the Yahagi bridge near Okazaki (below), Tōkichirō, as he was then still called, was spotted by a fortune teller, who prophesied the boy would one day inherit the realm. Another source claims Tōkichirō first came to Nobunaga's notice as a sandal bearer when on a cold winter's day, he helped his lord into sandals he had kept warm at his bosom.

From this humble position, Hideyoshi worked his way up to the head of the kitchen. From there he steadily climbed the ranks in Nobunaga's meritocracy until, in 1561, he married Nene, the daughter of one of Nobunaga's commanders, and was appointed commander of a unit of ashigaru. The wedding seems to have been a very plain affair, conducted on simple straw mats as one might find in the dwelling of commoners. Yet being of peasant stock himself, it cannot have bothered the warrior too much.

Akechi Mitsuhide (below) was born somewhere during the late 1520s. His father was the master of Akechi Castle and the chieftain of a small domain along the southern border of Mino province. Shortly after his coming-of-age ceremony, in 1545, Mitsuhide married Tsumaki Hiroko, the daughter of one of his vassals.

Mitsuhide spent his early years in the service of the Saitō clan, whose chieftain, Dōsan, had by then united Mino under his control. But in 1556, Dōsan was challenged by his eldest son Yoshitatsu. Father and son met each other in battle on the banks of the Nagara River. In this fight, the Akechi fought alongside Dōsan's forces, but they were defeated and nearby Akechi Castle fell into the hands of Yoshitatsu. Deprived of their family seat, Mitsuhide and his clan members fled across the border, into Echizen, where they were given refuge by the powerful Asakura.

It was not long afterward that Mitsuhide entered the service of Asakura Yoshikage, and for the next ten years served him in various capacities at his fortress of Ichijōdani. And it was at Ichijōdani, somewhere in the fall of 1566, that Mitsuhide first met the fugitive Ashikaga Yoshiaki, seeking to restore the Ashikaga *Bakufu* in the wake of the treacherous murder of his brother, Yoshikage, at the hands of Matsunaga and his henchmen. Over the next two years, they saw each other regularly and Mitsuhide became increasingly involved in Yoshiaki's ambition to restore the old order under an Ashikaga *Bakufu*.

The *Hosokawa kaki* describes how, on July 17, 1568, Mitsuhide traveled down to Inabayama Castle, where Oda Nobunaga had installed himself having subdued Mino. It was probably through his aunt, Ominokata, who had been married to Saitō Dōsan, that Mitsuhide was able to establish contact with Nobunaga, who was, after all, married to Ominokata and Dōsan's daughter, Nōhime. From then onward Mitsuhide served the interests of both Yoshiaki and Nobunaga, which were, for the next few years, at least, more-or-less aligned.

Nobunaga and his chief retainers: Shibata Katsuie (middle), Hashiba Hideyoshi (right), and Sakuma Nobumori (left)

Hideyoshi's first chance to make a serious impression comes in 1569 when Nobunaga puts him in charge of twenty thousand men to subdue Tajima province, the power boundary between the Oda and the Mōri. He passes the test with flying colors: within just ten days he subdues some eighteen castles. Over the next decade, he plays major roles in most of Nobunaga's major battles, against the Asakura and Asai at Ane River, against the Takeda at Nagashino, and against Matsunaga Hisahide at his last holdout of Shigisan Castle. Most of the last years of that decade, Hideyoshi spends in combatting the intransigent Mōri in western Honshū.

Akechi Mitsuhide also takes part in many of these battles. Yet his background is profoundly different from that of Hideyoshi. Born into a clan descended from the legendary Minamoto, Mitsuhide begins his military career by entering the service of Asakura Yoshikage. It is there that he is first introduced to Shōgun Ashikaga Yoshiaki, then still a fugitive seeking to restore power to the Shōgunate. Though hospitable, the Asakura balk at marching on the capital. And it is on Mitsuhide's advice and through his negotiations that Yoshiaki eventually comes to rely on Nobunaga. Yet as soon as he has installed Yoshiaki in the capital, Nobunaga begins to curtail his powers. And just as soon Yoshiaki begins to conspire against Nobunaga, so much so that in the summer of 1573, Nobunaga expelled him from the capital.

The Shōgun's deposition is the first crack in Mitsuhide's relationship with Nobunaga. Soon more cracks will appear.

Having rid himself of Yoshiaki, Nobunaga builds a vast fortress on the crest of Azuchi-*yama*, a high hill on the southern shore of Lake Biwa, some thirty miles from the capital. From there he begins to work towards the subjugation of western Japan. In the meantime, he receives a string of envoys

Azuchi Castle, with in the background Lake Biwa

Fighting at the Ishiyama Hongan-*ji*, a campaign that would consume almost a decade

from the imperial court in Kyoto, which in its own way seeks to curtail Nobunaga's drive towards centralized control by granting him a formal title. But Nobunaga isn't really interested; he wants total control to achieve his revolutionary objectives. For that purpose, he even builds an imperial residence on the grounds of his new castle.

For Mitsuhide, who has always believed in the old order, it is hard to accept Nobunaga's radical departure. Yet he also realizes his country's need for stability, a stability that can only be achieved by the likes of Nobunaga. And thus he continues to serve him tirelessly. They are hard years for the sensitive warrior, whose major pastime is to write poems over a cup of tea. At the end of May 1567, following a grueling campaign against the fanatics at the Ishiyama Hongan-*ji*, he collapses with fatigue is forced to take time off. That same year his beloved wife, Hiroko, dies after a short illness.

But soon Mitsuhide is back in the saddle, like Hideyoshi, spending the rest of the decade campaigning in western Honshū. For this, he is rewarded with the province of Tanba. It seems that (at least at this stage) Mitsuhide is grateful for Nobunaga's gesture, for on July 2, 1581, in a postscript to his clan's family code, he notes how: 'Nobunaga took a rolling stone like me and lifted me from obscurity, bestowing on me excessive favors. For this our clan's retainers, down to their distant descendants, should not forget their duty to our lord Nobunaga.' Mitsuhide's apparent devotion to his master does not go unnoticed. The Jesuit missionary Lois Fróis, who met Nobunaga on several occasions and thus also came to know his close retainers, observes how:

> More than anyone, Mitsuhide tirelessly plies Nobunaga with gifts, exploring all manner of means to please him and thus gain his affection, his heart bent on avoiding anything that might go against Nobunaga's wishes or tastes.

Nobunaga takes it out on Mitsuhide

And yet, at the same time, it seems that he often fails to please his master. The same Fróis goes on to describe how 'it is widely rumored that fol-

lowing an argument behind close doors Nobunaga kicked him twice.' Others too observe a masochistic streak in their relationship. Works like the *Sofu monogatari*, the *Akechi gunki*, and the *Kawasumi taikōki* all mention scenes in which an obsequious Mitsuhide is scolded by Nobunaga in front of others, the latter even claiming Nobunaga instructs his son to hit Mitsuhide over the head with an iron battle fan. The estrangement between the two is worsened by the death of Mitsuhide's younger sister, who is one of Nobunaga's favorite concubines. It almost naturally drives him to restore his support for Ashikaga Yoshiaki, who from his makeshift palace in Tomo, still seeks to enlist the support of warlords to restore the Muromachi *Bakufu*. At the same time, it may well be more exalted motives than a mere spanking from Nobunaga that drive Mitsuhide back into the arms of his former master. And in this he is not alone; except for visionaries like Ieyasu, only few of his contemporaries are able or willing to follow Nobunaga's vision for Japan to its ultimate consequence: a separation of warriors from their lands; a separation of church and state; the abolishment of the *Bakufu*—and all this below a powerless emperor!

Mitsuhide, then, has good reason to believe he will receive widespread support if he decides to move against Nobunaga. The question is: when? This question answers itself during the first week of June 1582, when Nobunaga orders Mitsuhide to act as master of ceremonies during a three-day-long banquet at Azuchi Castle in honor of Ieyasu for their successful three-year-long campaign against Takeda Katsuyori. Then, on June 7, a messenger arrives with a letter from Hideyoshi with an urgent request for assistance in his campaign against the intransigent Mōri at Takamatsu Castle. At this, according to the *Shinchō kōki*, Nobunaga exclaims, 'This is the perfect opportunity; I will ride out myself to destroy once and for all of all the chieftains in Chūgoku (western Honshū) and subjugate the whole region down to the island of Kyushu.' Over the next few days, Nobunaga continues to entertain Ieyasu, while Mitsuhide is ordered to return to his headquarters of Sakamoto Castle and raise a vanguard.

At this stage, it still seems Mitsuhide is indeed preparing to lead Nobunaga's vanguard toward Chūgoku. On June 16, he travels down to Kameyama Castle in Tanba, well on the way toward Chūgoku. Yet it is clear

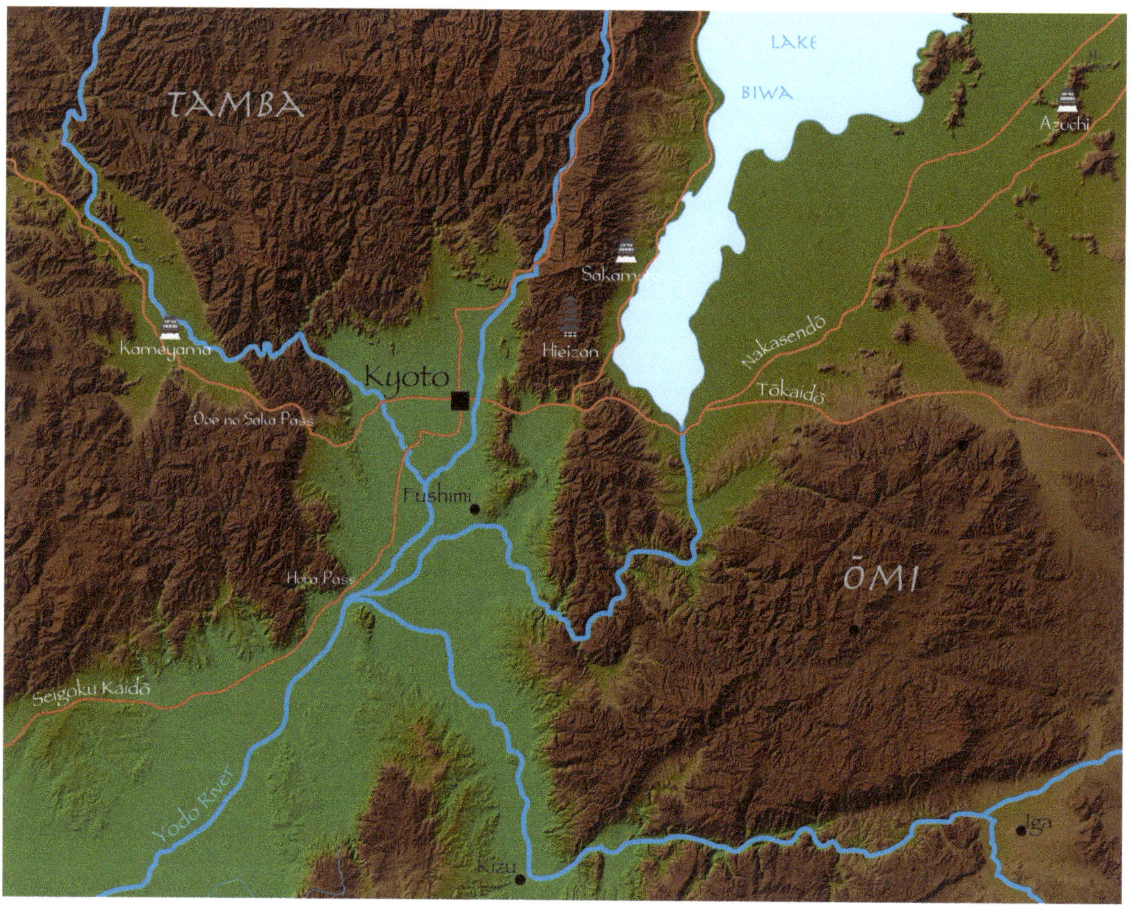

that by this time he is already secretly plotting against his master and benefactor. On his departure from Sakamoto Castle, he dispatches a messenger to Uozu in the northern province of Ettchu with a letter to one of Uesugi Kagekatsu's vassals, imploring him to 'tell your master to send the maximum number of men to our aid' (*go-tōhō muni gochisō mooshiageru*). He is clearly not acting alone; signing off on 'his highness's' behalf, Mitsuhide implies he is acting on behalf of none other than the deposed Shōgun.

The next day, June 17, Mitsuhide climbs Mount Atago, situated just north of his castle. There, at the Atago Shrine, overlooking the ancient capital, he offers prayers and stays for the night. The *Shinchō kōki* describes how, while staying at the shrine, Mitsuhide draws fortune slips (*o-mikuji*) up to three

Opposite page: Mount Atago, with the Atago Shrine at its crest

愛宕山
朝日峯
石和板

times. What goes through the warrior's head as he studies the cryptic predictions on the slips? Is he still weighing his loyalty towards his benefactor against his duty to restore the Ashikaga *Bakufu*? Or is he looking to revenge the insults he has suffered at Nobunaga's hands? His movements betray no such intentions. Two days later, back at Kameyama Castle, he dispatches a transport corps with a hundred cases of military supplies—bows, arrows, muskets, and ammunition—westward, toward Hideyoshi at Takamatsu Castle.

Nobunaga, meanwhile, orders his army to stand by for departure and travels up to the capital. There he installs himself at the Honnō Temple, his usual abode when he resides in Kyoto. He has only brought with him a small escort of guards. It is a departure from usual, for according to Fróis, whose Jesuit Mission is nearby, he is usually accompanied by a guard of two thousand men on horseback. Always apt to combine pleasure with duty, he uses the temple as a venue for a grand tea ceremony for which he has brought

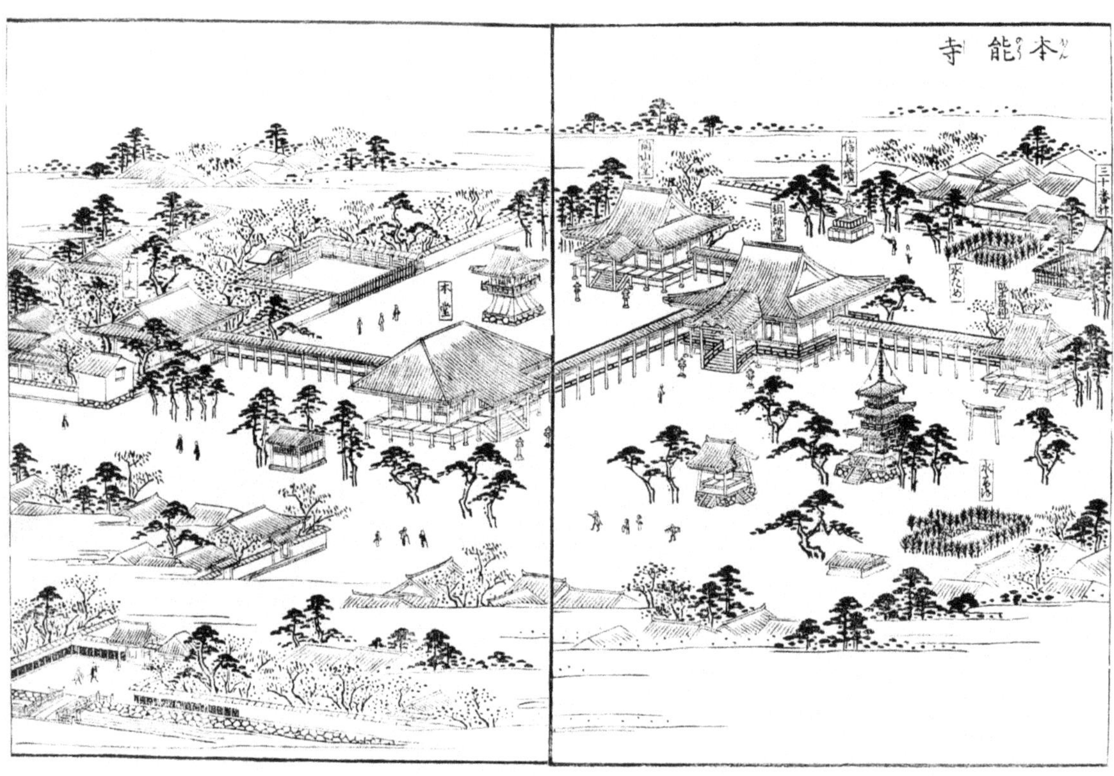

The Honnō Temple in Nobunaga's day

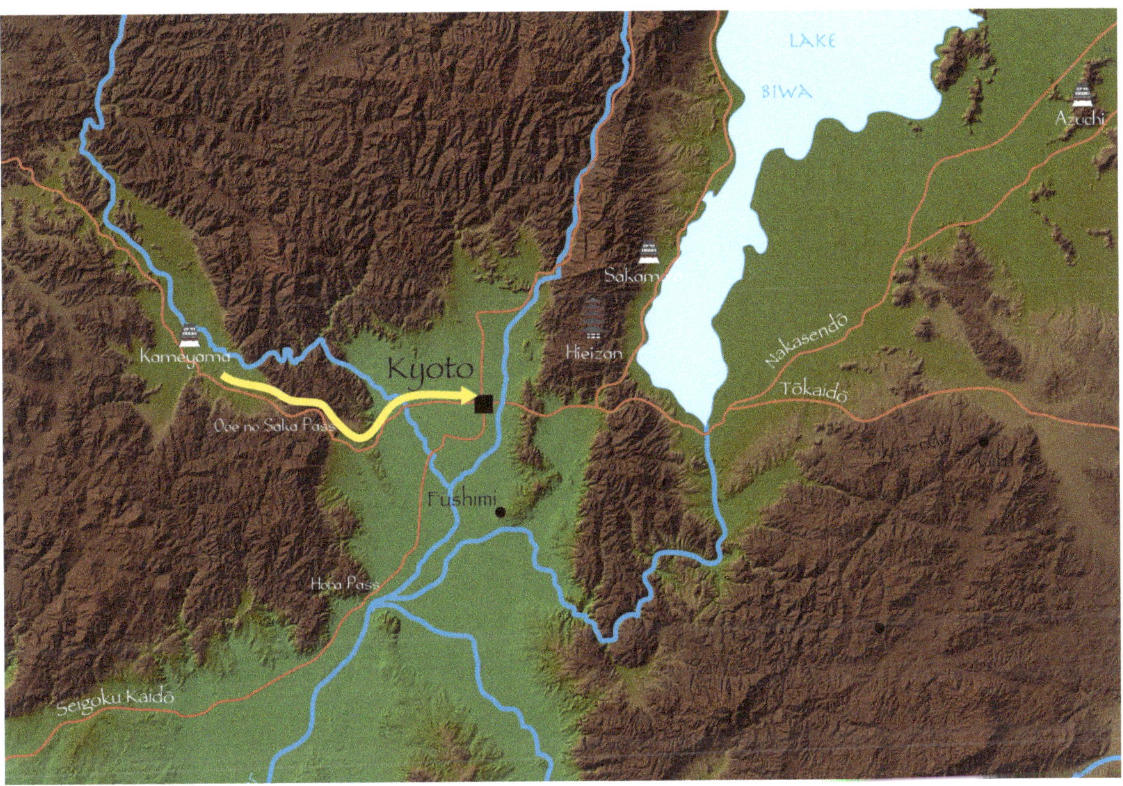

along some thirty-eight exquisite items to show off to his guests. The tea ceremony is given on June 20 and attended by some forty notables. Afterward, he attends a bout of *igo* (a game based on capturing territory) until late at night, when he finally turns in.

At this point, Mitsuhide has already departed from Kameyama Castle at the head of some thirteen thousand men. Yet he does not set out westwards to Chūgoku, but eastwards, to the capital where he knows Nobunaga is staying. At the hour of the rooster (5-6 o'clock in the afternoon) he reaches the foot of the Ooe no Saka Pass, the western gateway to the capital. There, at the Shinomura Hachiman Shrine, he sits down with his five chief vassals and reveals to them his plan to overthrow Nobunaga. All agree and sign a written vow to the gods they will see it through till the bitter end. Resting their horses and men they take some food. Then they mount their horses again and enter the pass.

Before dawn, they reach the Katsura River, on the western edge of the capital. Here Mitsuhide orders his men to halt again to remove the shoes the horses have worn to cross the pass, and for his ashigaru to put on a fresh pair of sandals. Then he proceeds to cut one-and-a-half foot lengths of fuse cord and, lighting them, orders his musketeers to suspend them from their belts in bundles of five strands at a time.

By the time they cross the bridge over the Katsura River, the sun has already risen. It is now June 21, 1582. Soon they are within the vicinity of the Honnō Temple. Kicking down the wicket gates that separate the neighborhood blocks, Mitsuhide's commander of the advance guard, Saitō Toshimitsu, splits his men into several groups that make their way toward the temple from all directions. By four o'clock in the morning, the hour of the Dragon, they have the temple completely surrounded. Being the designated place for Nobunaga to stay when visiting the capital, the temple has some defenses, including stone walls and a three yards wide moat, yet they are no match for Mitsuhide's troops, who have spent a decade of hard campaigning in sieges against high-walled strongholds. Nor is Nobunaga's guard in any way up to the task. Emerging from the stables and the first to face the intruders, his horse specialist, Yashiro Shōsuke and three others throw themselves on the attackers but are immediately killed. By this time Nobunaga and the rest

Nobunaga (right) and his men are under attack

Yasuda Kunitsugu attacks Nobunaga

of his guard have risen and barricade themselves as best they can in the goten, Nobunaga's official residence on the temple grounds. Nobunaga at first believed it was just his own men fighting among each other. But now he realizes his mistake. Turning to his eighteen-year-old attendant, Mori Ranmaru, who is dressed in no more than in a summer kosode, he exclaims, 'Well then, a rebellion; who is behind it?' The latter replies, 'I can see Akechi men!' At which Nobunaga remarks, '*Zehi ni oyobazu* (Such is life), the exact same words he spoke when he was betrayed by his brother-in-law, Azai Nagamasa, a dozen years earlier.

Mitsuhide's men, by then, have already crossed the forecourt and are forcing their way into the compound. At the kitchen entrance, they are met by Takahashi Toramatsu, who like Ranmaru is one of Nobunaga's close attendants. Armed with a lance, he puts up a stiff fight but is soon overwhelmed and dies on the spot. The next to fall is Ranmaru, struck in the lower abdomen by Yasuda Kunitsugu, one of Toshimitsu's lancers. Before long all thirty of those who are with Nobunaga on this fateful morning have perished. Nobunaga himself, too, puts up a stiff fight. Armed with a bow and arrow he kills a number of the assailants as they cross the wide forecourt. When the bow's string breaks, he grabs a lance and kills several more, until

Ranmaru fends off Yasuda Kunitsugu

he is struck in the elbow. His last orders are for the womenfolk to escape from the compound. Then, according to the *Shinchō kōki*, he withdraws 'into the inner recesses of the compound, which by now had caught fire and were ablaze throughout. And locking it from within he disemboweled himself.'

Lois Fróis, who is about to conduct early Mass at his Kyoto Mission, is stunned when his disciples rush in with the news of Nobunaga's death. Writing back home later, he reflects how:

> This man, who made everyone tremble, not just at the sound of his voice but even at the mentioning of his name, has been reduced to dust and ashes so that not even a small hair remains.

YAMASAKI

Nobunaga's death sends shockwaves through the realm. For a decade he has held central Japan in an iron grip, gradually working towards his aim to pacifying the whole country: *tenka fūbu*. Some welcomed his end. At court officials celebrate; they have come to loathe his disrespect for the emperor and his increased meddling in such minute details as the use of the intercalary month in Japan's Lunisolar calendar (which differs from region to region), a prerogative that has hitherto belonged solely to the imperial court. Within days of Nobunaga's death, they appoint Mitsuhide governor of Kyoto. Aware on which side his bread is buttered, Mitsuhide donates some five-hundred pieces of gold to the court. Meanwhile, he seeks to cash in on his newly gained position by rallying the factions that might help him to achieve his ultimate aim: to restore the Ashikaga *Bakufu*.

Ashikaga Yoshiaki himself, too, makes the most of Nobunaga's death. From Tomo he dispatches letters to sympathetic warlords throughout the realm, urging them to rise to the occasion and reinstall him as the rightful Shōgun, presenting events as though he himself has deposed his nemesis. Yet few warlords respond, either to Yoshiaki's appeals or those of Mitsuhide. They are nervous, as it is hard to decide how the cards will fall. Especially Mitsuhide's failure to produce Nobunaga's head makes them jittery. Who knows for sure if Nobunaga has not managed to make his escape in the flames

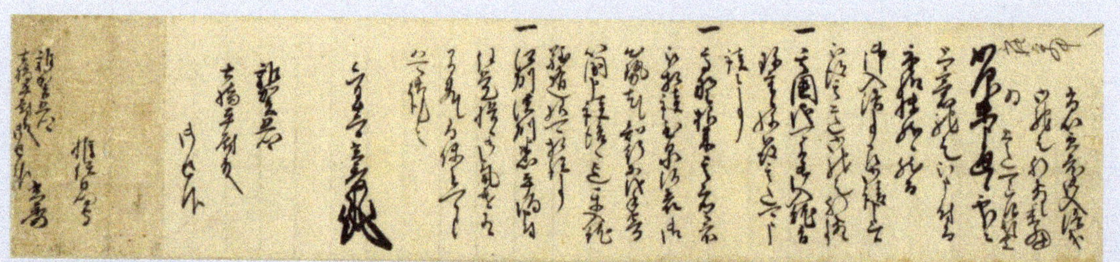

Mitsuhide's efforts to reinstate the Shōgun are again borne out by a recently discovered letter written ten days after the Honnō Incident and addressed to Tsuchibashi Shigeharu, a leader of the Saika Ikkō sectarians:

I apologize for not having written lately, yet I am grateful to hear you have been ordered to exert yourselves on His Majesty's behalf. However, there is already agreement on His Majesty returning to the capital. Hence it is of the utmost importance that you understand this and exert yourselves accordingly.

- *I am grateful that the Saika sectarians have chosen to join my side. And we should increasingly take this to heart and consult each other accordingly.*
- *I have also consulted with the Kōya, Negoro and Kaga sectarians and am delighted to see that they have mobilized their forces in the direction of Izumi and Kawachi. As with regards to the rewards, this should be worked out between you and my clan's elders, and done in such a manner that we will mutually benefit for many years to come.*
- *I have ordered my men to subdue Ōmi and Mino and in this, they have succeeded. There is no need to worry. What remains will be explained by my messenger.*

PS: It is of the utmost importance that you exert yourselves to escort His Majesty back to the capital. I cannot go into further detail here, as they will in time be explained by His Majesty himself.

and the confusion? Who knows whether he might not suddenly show up at the head of a mighty force to wreak the kind of revenge he unleashed on the monks at Hiezan? No, better to let others do the dangerous work. And thus they all stay put, waiting for the next move of the other major players on the political scene: Tokugawa Ieyasu and Hashiba Hideyoshi.

Ieyasu, at the time of Mitsuhide's attack on the Honnō Temple, has just been sightseeing at Sakai. Only two weeks have passed since he and Nobunaga were at Azuchi Castle celebrating their successful campaign against Takeda Katsuyori. It is on Nobunaga's invitation that he has gone down to Sakai to see the impressive *tekkōsen*, the ironclads that were used to such great effect against the Mōri fleet in the Bay of Osaka. He has been staying at the *yashiki* of Matsui Yūkan, a private secretary to Nobunaga, who entertains close relations to Sakai's rich merchants and has procured so many of the exquisite tea implements on behalf Nobunaga. He has just left Yūkan's *yashiki* and is on his way to rendezvous with Nobunaga at the Honnō Temple when, at noon, June 21, while resting at Shijōnawate, Kawachi province, just west of Osaka, he is met by Chaya Kiyonobu, a Sakai merchant who has long been in Ieyasu service and breaks to him the dramatic news to his master for the first time.

Like Nobunaga, Ieyasu is accompanied by some thirty retainers. As Nobunaga's chief ally he is keenly aware his life is in serious danger. For a moment he contemplates suicide—as he did in the wake of the Battle of Okehazama. But again he is dissuaded, this time not by a monk but by his old vassal, Honda Tadakatsu. It is another of his trusted retainers, Hattori Masa-

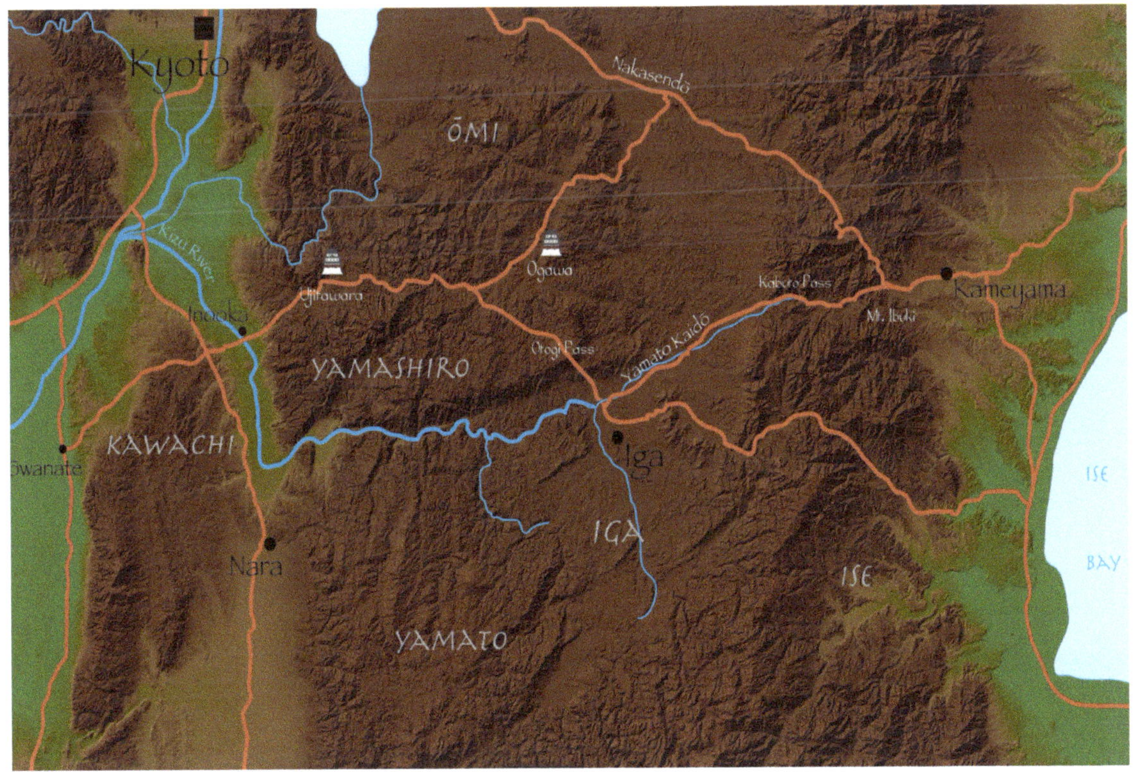

nari, whose ancestors hail from Iga, who persuades Ieyasu to try and reach Okazaki by crossing the heartlands of the Ise Peninsula. Another member of Ieyasu's party, Hasegawa Hidekazu, a Nobunaga retainer who has been acting as Ieyasu's guide, is befriended with chieftains in Yamashiro. And thus they set out for Inooka, where they intend to take the old ferry across the Kizu River, the natural border between Kawachi and Yamashiro. But on their way there, part of the small band of warriors begins to lag behind. It is to be their undoing. Just before they reach the western bank of the Kizu River, they are ambushed by a band of armed peasants, who mistake them for *ochimusha*. All of them are killed, including Anayama Nobutada, once one of Takeda Shingen's twenty-four generals fought at Kawanakajima, who has entered Ieyasu's service following his master's demise.

The rest of the party manages to safely make it to the other side, where Tadakatsu thrust his lance through the boat's hull to render it useless to their pursuers. They are met by a party sent by Yamaguchi Mitsuhiro, one of Hasegawa Hidekazu's friends in Yamashiro, who escorts them to Mitsuhiro's headquarters of Ujitawara Castle, in the Yamashiro heartlands, some fifteen miles west from where they landed.

The next day, June 22, escorted by Mitsuhiro's guards, they safely reach Ogawa Castle, across the border with Ōmi, where they are the guests of Mitsuhiro's father for the night. From there they head southward, crossing the Otogi Pass on the border with Iga by early noon. The *Mikawa monogatari* relates how, once in Iga, they are able to rely on Hattori Masanari's connections with local chieftains. As he had told Ieyasu, the locals are more than keen to offer him protection, despite his former alliance with Oda Nobunaga:

> When lord Nobunaga pacified the land of Iga, he put everyone to death, and those who fled abroad too were caught and killed. But Lord Ieyasu did not kill not even one of those who found their way to Mikawa. Instead, he helped them to rebuild their lives, so that those who later made their way back home never forgot, and were filled with gratitude for his help in their time of trouble and helped Ieyasu saying, 'we have to repay you out of our debt of gratitude.'

Opposite page: Anayama Nobutada, who lost his life on the banks of the Kizu River

甲越勇將傳
武田家廿四將
穴山伊豆守信良

From Ueno, they pick up the Yamato Kaidō towards the safety of the town of Kameyama. But that evening, while crossing the Kabuto Pass, they are set upon by Ikkō sectarians. They manage to drive them off with the help of Mitsuhiro's men, who have been ordered to accompany Ieyasu safely across Iga and Ise. And thus it is that the next day, Ieyasu and his men embark unharmed from the port of Nago and safely reach the port of Ōhama, just a few hours ride south from Okazaki Castle.

No sooner has Ieyasu reached Okazaki than he begins to assemble an army to punish Mitsuhide. But he has already been outmaneuvered. Down in Bittchū, Hashiba Hideyoshi has also learned of Mitsuhide's treachery. For well over a month now, he has been trying to reduce Takamatsu Castle. It is the stronghold of Shimizu Muneharu, an ally of the powerful Mōri, who control much of western Honshū. Soon the rainy season will be upon them, causing the nearby Ashimori River to swell to a mighty river. Putting his men to work, Hideyoshi makes them erect a twenty feet high dam that stretches for more than two miles across the river's estuary. When the rain finally comes, the river bursts its banks, flooding the surrounding area, which consists largely of low-lying paddy fields, and reducing Takamatsu Castle to a small island in a vast lake. But the castle's five thousand defenders stub-

The siege of Takamatsu Castle

Hideyoshi (bottom left corner) overseas the siege

bornly hold out. To make matter worse, the Mōri have come to Muneharu's aid with a force twice that of Hideyoshi. He had already sent a request for reinforcements to Nobunaga, but except for some spearhead supplies from Mitsuhide he has so far received none.

Then, on the night of June 22, his men intercept a secret messenger. It is a stroke of extremely good luck. The messenger carries a letter from none other than Mitsuhide, saying he intends to move against Nobunaga and encouraging the Mōri to hold out so they can deal with Hideyoshi together. Hideyoshi is stunned, not only by Mitsuhide's treachery but also because it puts him in a very dangerous position. Already he has trouble fighting the Mōri; if Mitsuhide moves against him from the east, he will be pincered between two forces. Keeping the news secret by imposing a gagging order on his men, he immediately sues for peace with the intransigent Mōri, promising them favorable conditions if they align themselves with him. His only condition is that Shimizu Muneharu should commit *seppuku*. The latter accepts, and as soon as the deed is done, Hideyoshi orders his army to lift the siege and ride eastward, toward Himeji.

Setting out from Takamatsu Castle in early in the afternoon of 25 June, they travel along the Sanyōdō throughout the night without rest and at such

Shimizu Muneharu, ready to give his life to reach a truce

a breakneck speed that they reach Himeji before dusk has set in the next evening—they have covered the fifty miles stretch in less than a day. By now the rainy season has begun and though the weather is atrocious, their task has been lightened by Hideyoshi's decision to transport the provisions and arms over the Inland Sea toward the port of Akashi. Known as the Chūgoku Daigaeshi, or the Great Return from Chūgoku, this remarkable feat is the most impressive forced march in Japanese military history.

Meanwhile, in an effort to win time to deal with the wayward rebel, Hideyoshi does all he can to spread the idea that Mitsuhide has failed in his pan. While still at Takamatsu, he begins writing letters (in person) to chieftains in the Home Provinces around the capital (many of whom are under

Mitsuhide's control). One of them is Nakagawa Kiyohide, the master of Ibaraki castle in Settsu:

June 24,
To Nakagawa Kiyohide,

Just as I was about to write to you I received your letter, which satisfied me no end.

Well then, I can tell you that I have just had clear confirmation from a messenger sent down from Kyoto: Lord Nobunaga and master Nobutada are safe and sound and were able to extricate themselves from Akechi Mitsuhide's attack. On their way to Zesegasaki in Ōmi, Fukutomi Hidekatsu attacked Mitsuhide's men up to three times. He has acquitted himself so well that I am delighted to be able to tell you that both father and son are well.

I myself will return to Himeji Castle at the earliest opportunity and will report back to you in good order, so please stand by.

Equally, it is of the utmost importance that you on your side, too, do everything in your power to counter Mitsuhide's forces.

Yours sincerely,
Hashiba Chikuzen Hideyoshi

It is a piece of counterintelligence that would have made Nobunaga smile—Hideyoshi has come a long way from his days as a sandal bearer.

By the time Hideyoshi returns to his headquarters of Himeji Castle in the

Hideyoshi moves his troops in the Chūgoku Daigaeshi

evening of June 26, he knows better. Nobunaga is dead, treacherously slain by one of his closest retainers. So is Nobunaga's oldest son, Nobutada, who likewise committed *seppuku* at the nearby and newly constructed Nijiō Castle after he has made sure the womenfolk and children have escaped.

Hideyoshi is determined to punish Mitsuhide. Assembling his commanders at his goten on the grounds of Himeji Castle, he denounces the callous treachery of Mitsuhide, a man who like himself has been raised from obscurity by the great Nobunaga. The next battle, he assures them, will be more than a just fight; it will be nothing less than a *tomurai kassen*, a 'memorial battle' in honor of Nobunaga. Shrewd operator as he is, he also makes sure not only to satisfy their moral sense of outrage. Opening Himeji's vaults, he distributes its total store of gold and silver among them. Over the next few days, as they rest and await his ships to arrive in Akashi, he pampers his allies with good food and goes out of his way to win their long-lasting support—he is already thinking ahead, to his position after he has dealt with Mitsuhide.

Hideyoshi's headquarters of Himeji Castle

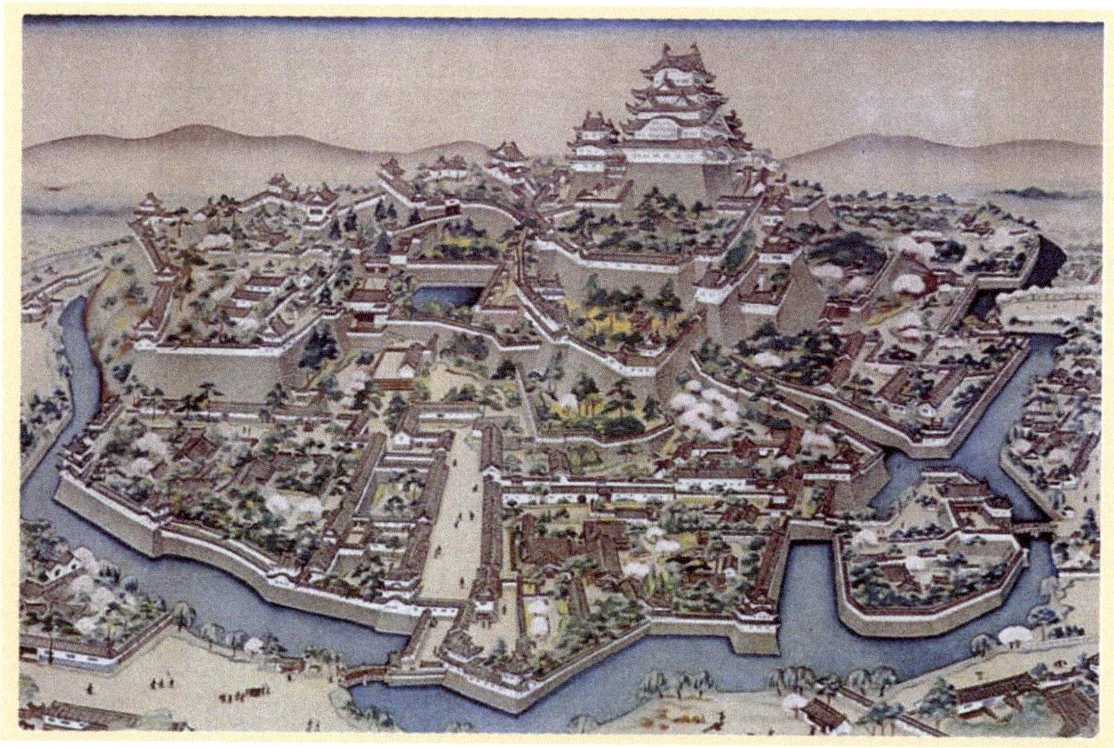

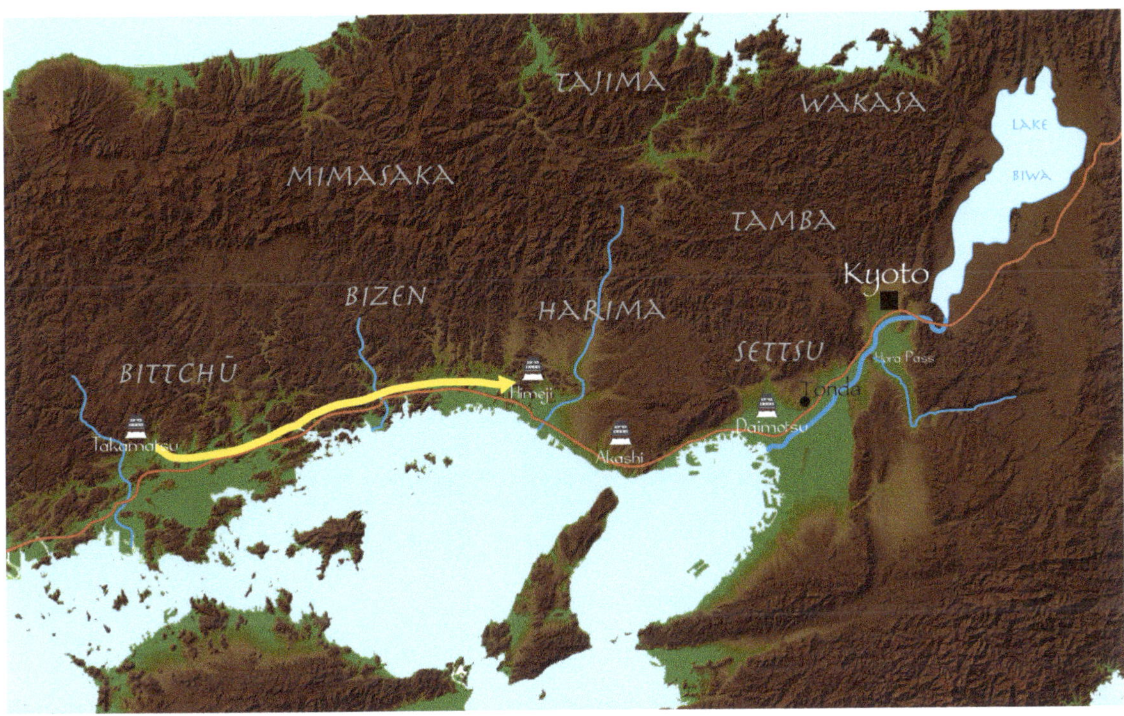

Departing from Himeji on June 28, Hideyoshi marches for the port town of Akashi, where his supplies from Takamatsu have meanwhile arrived. From there he and his army of roughly eight thousand men proceed eastward, toward the Bay of Hyōgo, where they pitch camp for the night. By this time his spies have informed him that Mitsuhide is holding up in the vicinity of Fushimi, just south of the capital, and that he has moved some of his troops towards the village of Yamasaki, situated at the strategic narrow of the Hora Pass. Pincered between Mount Tennō and the point where the Katsura, Uji, and Kizu Rivers join together to form the majestic Yodo River, the pass—which isn't high but very narrow—is the main western gateway to the capital.

By the evening of the last day of June, Hideyoshi has reached Daimotsu Castle, which stands on the northern bank of the Yodo River and looks out over the sprawling city of Osaka on the other side. By now his army has swollen to a mighty force. His moral appeal, together with his ability to cajole them, has caused chieftains throughout the region to respond to his call to right the wrong that has been perpetrated and play their part in Nobunaga's

Daimotsu Castle, with in the foreground the Yodo River

memorial battle. Kuroda Yoshitaka was already on board, but now Hori Hidemasa also throws in his lot with Hideyoshi.

Mitsuhide, meanwhile, hasn't added a single man to his army. He had banked on allies to join him. One of them is Tustsui Junkei. In the immediate aftermath of the rebellion, he helped Mitsuhide quell much of Ōmi. His headquarters of Kōriyama Castle stands only ten miles south of the Hora Pass. But Junkei doesn't move. He too has received a letter from Hideyoshi. And though he does not respond to Hideyoshi's overtures, neither does he come to Mitsuhide's aid. Even Mitsuhide's longstanding ally, Hosokawa Fujitaka and his son, Tadaoki, who has married Mitsuhide's daughter, Tama, fail to respond to his repeated requests for assistance. Instead, they shave their heads, take Buddhist names, and go into mourning. Not willing to divorce

Opposite page: A shaven Hosokawa Fujitaka

大日本六十余将
丹後
細川兵部大輔藤孝
春亭京雀記

his wife—now the daughter of a traitor—Tadaoki sends Tama into exile in the village of Midono on the Tango Peninsula. Even when Mitsuhide offers them the provinces of Settsu, as well as Tajima and Wakasa, they refuse. Of course, they too have meanwhile been forewarned by Hideyoshi. The latter is of course delighted. He immediately writes them another letter, thanking them for their 'over-all cooperation,' adding a written vow assuring them 'favorable conditions' once the dust has settled—they needn't join him, as long as they don't join his enemy. That same evening, June 30, he goes down to the nearby Seiken Shrine and likewise has his head shaved.

At noon, the following day, Hideyoshi arrives at Tonda, some six miles west of the Hora Pass. While his men set up camp the ground continues to reverberate with the rumbling of hoofs plowing ground; more chieftains who have responded to Hideyoshi's relentless barrage of letters descend on Tonda. Ikeda Tsuneoki, Nakagawa Kiyohide, Takayama Ukon all join him, multiplying his army to over twenty-four thousand men.

That evening, Hideyoshi calls his allies and generals to a lengthy war council, in which he suggests overall command should go to Niwa Nagahide, a senior veteran from Nobunaga's ranks. But Nagahide refuses. Is this battle,

Hideyoshi and his generals convene a war council

he argues, not to be a memorial battle? What would be more fitting, then, than to appoint as supreme commander Nobunaga's surviving son, Nobutaka, who is still underway with some four thousand men? Hideyoshi approves, though on everyone's insistence he assumes overall control of the alliance.

Resigning to his fate, Mitsuhide has meanwhile dispersed his troops at the eastern entrance to the pass, hoping to chip away at his Hideyoshi's forces as they exit Yamasaki. Short on men, he requisitions part of the local peasantry to help reinforce Shōryūji Castle, which has partially been destroyed by Nobunaga. He sets up his headquarters at an old burial mound halfway the pass and the castle, just two miles northeast of the pass.

First hostilities begin in the dead of night when a unit of musketeers under the command of Matsuda Masachika scale the eastern slope of the mountain. It results in some desultory exchanges of fire, but they are out-

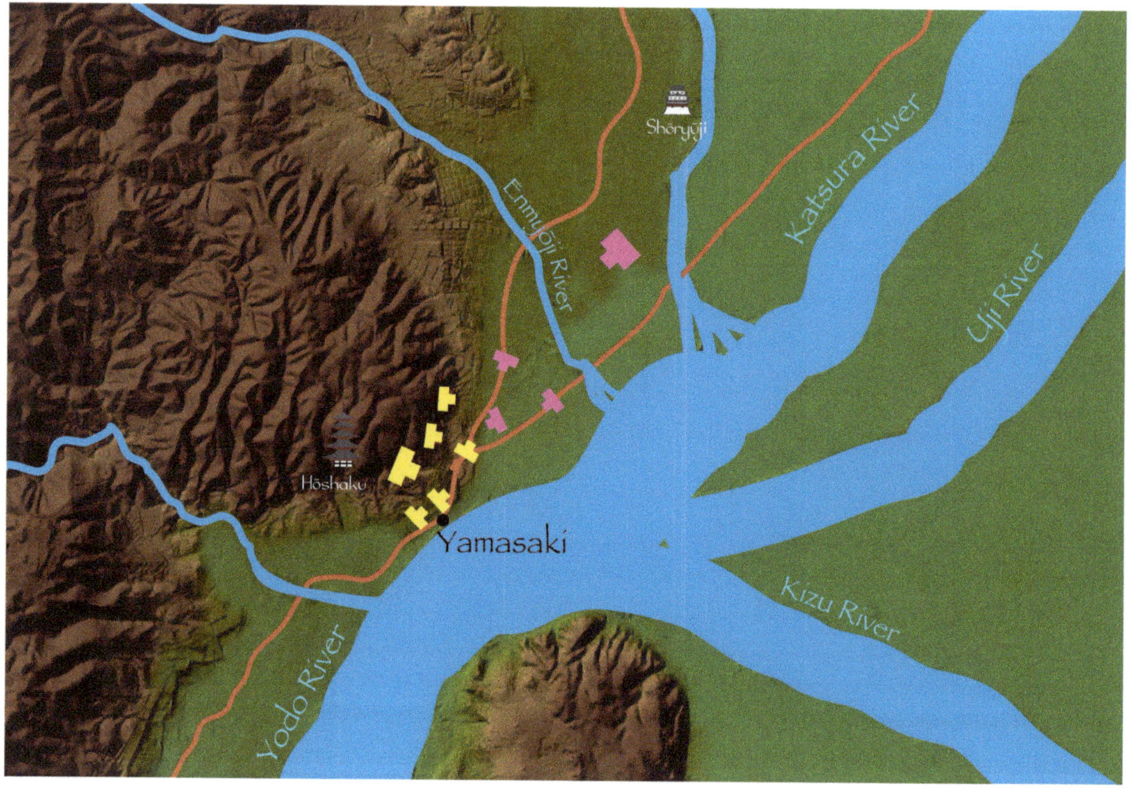

numbered and eventually thrown back by units under the command of Hori Hidemasa and Nakagawa Kiyohide.

The next day, July 2, 1582, Hideyoshi sets up his headquarters at the Hōshaku Temple, on the southern slope of Mount Tennō. The rain is still pouring down hard and fast, making it difficult to take stock of Mitsuhide's positions. Part of his own army has taken up positions at the foot of the mountain; the rest has been dispersed close along the northern bank of the raging Yodo River. He is still waiting for Nobutaka to arrive and assume his symbolic role of supreme commander. Down below Takayama Ukon is moving his men along the narrow Saigoku Highroad through Yamasaki when part of Mitsuhide's spearhead division is trying to break down the gate at the opposite end of the village. He immediately orders his men to attack. Ukon is joined by Nagagawa Kiyohide and Ikeda Tsuneoki, and together they force Mitsuhide's spearhead to withdraw behind the Enmyōji River (today's

(Koizumi River), a small tributary to the Yodo River descending from the southern slopes of Mount Tennō.

Soon all fighting concentrates along the banks of the Enmyōji River. Unhampered by Mitsuhide's spearhead, one unit after another now pushes through Yamasaki's narrow main street, pouring out on the widening plain and joining the others to throw themselves on the enemy. Partly out of lack of motivation, partly overwhelmed by the superior numbers of the enemy, Mitsuhide's army soon begins to fall apart and retreat. From his elevated position on the burial mound, Mitsuhide can only watch as his troops rush past him. He now realizes he has made a fatal mistake: he hasn't fixed a rallying point, enabling his men to fall back and reassemble. Instead, they split up in two directions, those from Kameyama Castle towards Tanba, those from Sakamoto towards Ōmi. The remainder flees towards Kyoto, trying to find refuge there by laying low. But the townspeople have closed the capital's gates and refuse to let them in for fear of fighting in the capital.

One of Mitsuhide's retainers and generals, Mimaki Kaneaki, realizing the hopelessness of their situation, resolves to make a last valiant stand so as to save the life of his master. And thus he dispatched a messenger to Mitsuhide, saying that he will fend off the enemy long enough for Mitsuhide to retreat.

Hideyoshi's warriors engage with the enemy

瓢軍談五十四場
三十四
旧臣等
道秀の討死を
諫る

Hideyoshi's warriors pursue their enemy into the Enmyōji River

Then he takes two hundred mounted warriors and rushed headlong into the advancing wall of enemy warriors. The *Taikō-ki* describes how:

> Kaneaki and his warriors fought with great spirit. Alas, fighting the enemy with only a few men, they were like a drop in the ocean, a single hair among a herd of cows, and within moments they were overwhelmed, so that not a man was left alive.

By now only some five thousand men are still with Mitsuhide on the burial mound. And it is with these that he now prepares to launch a final desperate assault on the enemy, when another retainer, Hida Tatewaki, seizes the reins of his horse and shouts:

> 'Our enemy is too strong and they outnumber us greatly, while half of our allies have abandoned us. This is not a situation in which you can hope to launch an attack! Now is the time to withdraw to Shōryūji Castle and try to temporarily hold out there!'

Opposite page: Mitsuhide is persuaded to withdraw

Following Tatewaki's advice and withdrawing to Shōryūji Castle,

Mitsuhide at first plans to hold out there. By now his army has shriveled to just seven hundred men. By the evening Hideyoshi's vastly superior army has the castle surrounded. As night sets in, Mitsuhide realizes the castle too is lost. Assembling his close retainers, he makes his escape from the castle at midnight and flees eastward, toward his stronghold of Sakamoto Castle. They get as far as Ogurisu, a small hamlet in the vicinity of Fushimi. There he is ambushed by a gang of *otona hyakushō*, armed peasants. They are bounty hunters, who make their living hunting down *ochimusha*, defeated warriors fleeing the scene of battle.

The *Taikō-ki* describes how, passing through a dense bamboo grove in file:

> Murakoshi Sanjūrō, who was upfront, was struck by a *yari* from the grove. Yet it failed to penetrate his sturdy *dōmaru* armor. But when Mitsuhide, who was the second mounted warrior, passed the grove, the weapon deeply entered his right-hand flank. At this, his companions drew up beside him and shouted, 'How dare you attack your allies! We will punish you severely!'

Mitsuhide and his retainers make their escape from Shōryūji Castle (right)

Mitsuhide is ambushed

But answer comes from the grove, saying they are not allies. Then follows a confused exchange among the assailants:

> 'There are five or six mounted men and only one or two attendants on foot! They're not ordinary warriors. They're clearly *ochimusha*, no need to ask! Blow the horn and assemble the men!'

Within moments the men on horseback are pursued by a large group of armed peasants accompanied by vicious dogs who snap at their feet. All of them are armed with spears and keen to claim their prize. Spurring on their horses, Mitsuhide and his men escape and finally find refuge among another bamboo grove. Grabbing the hand of one of his clansmen by the name of Mizo'o Katsubei Shigetomo, Mitushide tells him to inspect his wound. Katsubei bows his head: the wound is mortal. Accepting his fate, Mitsuhide instructs Katsubei to act as his *kaishaku*, to cut off his head the moment he has plunged his dagger into his lower abdomen. They are to bury his body but Katsubei is to burn his head and inter the ashes at the Chion Monastery, where they will be safe from Hideyoshi's men.

Mitsuhide (left) has handed his parting poem to Katsubei to read

Then, as he makes ready to take his life, Mitsuhide musters his last energy to compose his parting poem:

> There is only one way for those
> who follow the Way of the Warrior.
> Now, as I come to wake up
> from my fifty-five years' illusion,
> I will return to my roots.

Meanwhile, Mitsuhide's son-in-law, Hidemitsu, has made it back to Sakamoto Castle, where he is almost immediately besieged by Hori Hidemasa, who has been in hot pursuit from Yamasaki. Hidemitsu and his warriors hold out for another day until their position becomes untenable. The Kawasumi taikō-ki describes how, the next day:

> Hidemitsu takes his father-in-law's prized possessions and lowers them from the castle's donjon, where he and the rest of his clan are holding up, shouting, 'Give these to your Lord, Hidemasa. They are Mitsuhide's divine implements and no one should try to make them their own. Were I to let them perish with us I would stand accused of being an insolent fellow!' Before long Hidemasa made his appearance, saying, It is as you say. Yet why is it that Lord Mitsuhide's prized *wakizashi* by master smith Yoshihiroe from Kurikara is not among them?' At this Hidemitsu made answer, 'It is because it was given to Mitsuhide by Lord Nobunaga. As you yourself know all too well, the *wakizashi* forged by Yoshihiro was formerly worn by Lord Asakura Yoshikage when he conquered Echizen and it came into Mitsuhide's possession when he inquired about it afterward. I would like to hand it to you, but since Mitsuhide treasured it with all his life, I intend to wear it myself and return it to him when I meet him when I climb the mountain of the afterlife.

A somewhat formal depiction of the transfer of Mitsuhide's heirloom

Hideyoshi recognizes Mitsuhiude's features

On the evening of June 4, Hidemitsu, together with his wife and children as well as Mitsuhide's wife and children withdraw to the castle's upper chambers. There he and his close retainers put the women and children to death. Then, having set fire to the castle, Hidemitsu cuts open his belly and expires.

That same evening, a lone peasant makes his way towards Ōtsu, on the southern shore of Lake Biwa. It is where Hideyoshi, who has meanwhile pushed ahead towards Ōmi, is resting at the Onjō Temple. The peasant carries the severed head of Akechi Mitsuhide, wrapped in a waistcloth. During a *kubi jikken* Hideyoshi and his generals inspect the head along those of other killed enemy chieftains. There is no mistaking; it is Mitsuhide's head; Hideyoshi instantly recognizes the refined features of the man alongside whom he has fought so many battles on Nobunaga's behalf.

Following the ceremony, Hideyoshi orders Mitsuhide's head to be taken to the capital and to be put on display at the Honnō Temple, the place of his undoing. Two days later the head is impaled on a long spike and placed at Awataguchi, one of the seven ancient entries to the capital. Over the next weeks, people come from far and wide away to stand and gaze at the head of the man who ruled for just thirteen days.

SHIZUGATAKE

Having defeated Akechi Mitsuhide's forces at Yamasaki and displayed his head at the capital's eastern gate, Hideyoshi is now poised to take over the reins of his former lord and master Oda Nobunaga. But before he can effectively do so he faces one more obstacle: Shibata Katsuie. As one of the Oda clan's longstanding retainers, Katsuie wields considerable influence among the surviving members of the Oda clan, an influence that is strengthened when he marries Nobunaga's beautiful sister, Oichi no Kata, the former wife of Azai Nagamasa.

The rivalry between Hideyoshi and Katsuie is clearly on display soon after Nobunaga's death when, on July 16, 1582, Nobunaga's retainers gather at Kiyosu Castle to decide on who should succeed him. Hideyoshi favors Sanbōshi, the firstborn to Nobunaga's oldest son, Nobutada, who like his father has perished in the Honnō Rebellion. Ostensibly it is because Sanbōshi is Nobunaga's true legitimate heir, but given the boy is still in his infancy, it also gives Hideyoshi more leeway to decide on policy matters. For similar self-serving reasons Katsuie favors Nobunaga's third son, Nobutaka, for whom he has acted as guardian. In the end, however, Hideyoshi gets his way, partly because it has been he who has defeated Mitsuhide at Yamasaki, partly because he cleverly makes a number of concessions to appease his influential opponent.

Hideyoshi holds Sanbōshi at the Kiyosu Kaigi (meeting)

One of these concessions is to let Katsuie's adopted son, Katsutoyo, become the new master of Nagahama Castle in Ōmi. On the face of it, it seems a heavy concession to make. Built by Hideyoshi in 1573, and overlooking the eastern shore of Lake Biwa, it stands on the former domain of Azai Nagamasa. It had been Hideyoshi's role in the latter's demise that had earned him the domain. Three years it has taken him to build the castle, the materials for which have largely come from the ruins of Odani Castle. Like that castle, it controls traffic along the Hokuriku Kaidō, the old highroad into Japan's northern regions. For Katsuie, whose power base of Kitanoshō Castle is situated in Fuchū, in the province of Echizen, control over Nagahama Castle means unhampered access to the capital.

That Hideyoshi has no intention of sacrificing his former castle becomes apparent in the winter of that same year when, on December 26, he marches into Ōmi and lays siege to Nagahama Castle. It is a shrewd move, as he knows that the young and inexperienced Katsutoyo is on poor terms with his adoptive father, who, moreover, is tied down in Echizen by deep layers of snow. It isn't surprising, then, that Katsutoyo surrenders the castle within only a few days. Having regained his former castle, Hideyoshi now marches on Nobutaka's headquarters of Gifu Castle, doing the same there.

Shibata Katsuie was a longstanding retainer of the Oda clan. Born in 1522, he entered the service of Nobunaga's father, Nobuhide, at a young age. Following Nobuhide's death he became a counselor to his youngest son, Nobuyuki, joining the latter at Inou when he made battle with his older brother. But following Nobuyuki's defeat, Katsuie accepted Nobunaga's leadership of the Oda clan. And when Nobuyuki again conspired to overthrow his brother, it was Katsuie who revealed the plot to Nobunaga, who had his brother put to death. Katsuie was pardoned and entered Nobunaga's service, though the latter seemed to have made little use of it at first and Katsuie did not play a significant role in the Battle of Okehazama. By the end of the sixties, however, he had climbed to the position of bugyō (magistrate).

It seems Nobunaga had by then spotted Katsuie's martian as well as his administrative talents, for he not only took part in a number of battles but also became one of five councilors appointed to administer the Kinai region (after Nobunaga had installed Ashikaga Yoshiaki as *Shōgun*). The next years saw him take part in a great number of battles and sieges, at Noda Castle, at Fukushima Castle, at Ane River, at Ichijōdani Castle, and at Odani Castle, often leading the vanguard.

As Nobunaga's power grew, so did Katsuie's role grow in importance. By 1576 he had been appointed commanding officer of the Hokuriku region. It was in that capacity that, the next year, he took part in Nobunaga's campaign against Uesugi Kenshin (Battle of Tedori River). The next years saw him take part in yet more campaigns, mainly against the Ikkō sectarians in Kaga and Ettchū. By this time he had become one of Nobunaga's chief ministers.

1582, too, was a year filled with military campaigns in the north, all of them against Uesugi strongholds, including Matsukura Castle and Uozu Castle. And it was on June 25, three days after he had reduced Uozu Castle, that word reached Katsuie that his lord and master Nobunaga had been treacherously slain by one of his generals, Akechi Mitsuhide.

Meanwhile, Katsuie does not sit still either. Preparing to advance on Hideyoshi from the north, he mobilizes powerful allies to attack Hideyoshi in the rear. One of these is Takigawa Kazumasu, another Oda retainer who now begins to attack castles in Ise and installs himself at Nagashima Castle on the border between Ise and Owari. Faced with this threat, Hideyoshi is forced to move part of his army south into Ise to Kokufu Castle and from there move against Kazumasa at Nagashima Castle. But the Takigawa men offer fierce resistance and Hideyoshi is unable to do the same with Nagashima Castle. By now it is well into March of the next year and the snow has melted. Only weeks later, towards the end of April, word from Nagahama Castle reaches Hideyoshi at Gifu: Katsuie is moving into northern Ōmi along the Hokuriku Highroad at the head of some thirty thousand men.

Nagahama Castle

Leaving ten thousand men behind under the command of Nobunaga's second son, Nobukatsu, Hideyoshi leads the bulk of his force—some fifty thousand strong—up the Hokuriku Highroad, expecting to meet Katsuie in battle. On May 10, he sets up camp at Kinomoto, a hamlet on the northern outskirts of Nagahama, where the Hokuriku Kaidō emerges from the Ibuki Mountains and enters the alluvial plain along the eastern shore of Lake Biwa. It is the perfect place to block Katsuie's advance. But Katsuie fails to appear. He has set up camp at Yanagase, a post station along the same high road ten miles north from Kinomoto. And thus Hideyoshi sets out to repeat what Nobunaga did at Nagashino: to turn the terrain to his advantage. He first sets his men to work to erect a barrier across the highroad, running from the foot of Mount Dōgi on the west to Mount Tōno on the east. Atop this mountain stand the remains of Tōno Castle, the former citadel of the Tōno, a clan who held sway in the region during the second half of the previous

Hideyoshi's men take up their various positions

century. And it is here that Hideyoshi installs himself as he awaits Katsuie's attack.

Meanwhile, his generals do the same with the crests of other mountains, turning them into fortified bastions from which to counter the pending threat—Nakagawa Kiyohide at Mount Ooiwa, Takayama Ukon at Mount Iwasaki, and Kuwayama Shigeharu at Mount Shizugatake. They go at their task with such rigor that within a week they have turned the area into a heavily fortified bastion against an attack from the north. Yet even after a week of waiting Katsuie fails to launch his long-awaited assault. By the middle of May, Hideyoshi has lost patience and moves part of his army back to Nagahama Castle. That he is hoping to elicit an attack, is borne out by a short memo dated the last day of March (May 21) and addressed to his brother, Hashiba Hidenaga, instructing the latter:

> Move your men stationed outside the barricades around our fortifications inside. You and your men should help to tear down the huts of Shibata Katsutoyo's men, and Hori Hidemasa, Maeno Nagayasu, Kuroda Yoshitaka, and Kimura Shigekore too should busy themselves to get it all done before the day is out. Likewise, Tsutsui Junkei and

Hidemasa should vacate the area, so that tomorrow, the first day of April, we can move our men behind the trenches in question.

Two more weeks pass without any action from Katsuie. Then, on June 6, word reaches Hideyoshi that Oda Nobutaka has raised another army and is marching on Gifu in an apparent attempt to recapture his former stronghold. And thus Hideyoshi moves part of his army into Mino to intercept Nobukata before he can reach Gifu. But by now the rainy season has started and the Ibi River has burst its banks, forcing Hideyoshi to install himself at Ōgaki Castle and wait till the water levels have receded, thus giving Nobukata the time to recapture Gifu Castle.

It is at this junction, with part of Hideyoshi's army still engaged in the siege of Nagashima Castle in Ise and part of it waiting at Ōgaki Castle in

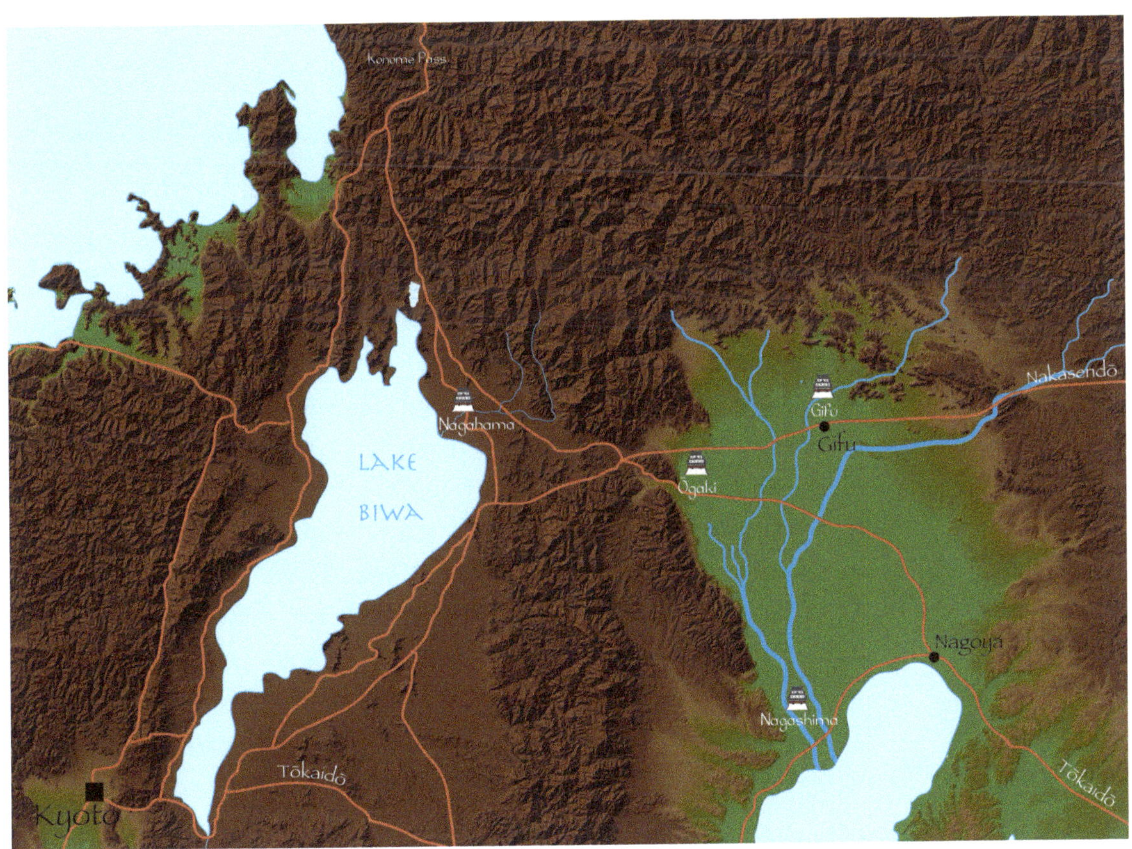

Mino, that Katsuie seizes his chance and orders the attack. The *Taikō-ki* describes how he does so on the strong urging of the redoubtable Sakuma Morimasa. like his cousin Katsuie, Morimasa is an Oda retainer of great standing, who played a significant role in Nobunaga's campaign to quell the Ikkō sectarians. Morimasa's plan is the brainchild of his commander, Masaji Masakuni, whom he has brought along and who argues that:

> 'All our enemy's forts put in place to subdue our forces are well manned and impenetrable. However, Nakagawa Kiyohide's fort on the other side of Lake Yogo consists of mainly tiny defenses that are removed from the rest of our enemy. Their buildings, too, are insubstantial. If we attack them there, the enemy will not expect us, and we will have the advantage of surprise. If we manage to surprise them we are certain to succeed, especially now Hideyoshi is away in Mino.'

Partly because he is tired of the standoff, partly because he has run out of options, Katsuie is eventually convinced and gives his approval. He sends Morimasa on his way with the words:

> 'I will keep the pressure on Hori Hidemasa's fortress, so you can safely launch your attack. However, when you withdraw afterward, as you must, you should do so in a straight line along the Hokuriku Kaidō, and refrain from setting up camp and settle in. So make sure you withdraw your troops before the day is out!'

And thus, on June 9, Morimasa leads his men westward, around Lake Yogo, and launches a withering assault on the troops of Nakagawa Kiyohide atop Mount Ooiwa. Kiyohide and his warriors offer fierce resistance, but after four hours of intense fighting, they aren't able to hold the fort and Kiyohide dies in its defense.

Having taken the fort on Mount Ooiwa, Morimasa now leads his men up the slopes of Mount Iwasaki, immediately north of Mount Ooiwa, forcing Takayama Ukon and his men to relinquish their fort atop the mountain and join Hashiba Hidenaga at Kinomoto. By now dusk has set in; they should retreat as Katsuie ordered. But Morimasa is drunk with the sweet taste of victory and decides to stay. He orders his men to settle in for the night atop

Morimasa's troops attacks Mount Ooiwa

Detail of the previous image: Nakagawa Kiyohide (center) makes his last stand

Mount Iwasaki. He knows that in doing so he goes against the explicit directions of Katsuie, but he refuses to give up on what he has conquered, even after Katsuie has sent over three messengers to remind him.

Emboldened by his success, the next day, June 10, Morimasa moves against Kuwayama Shigeharu at Mount Shizugatake. Shigeharu, too, is unable to withstand Morimasa's assault and orders his men to retreat. But somewhere halfway towards Kinomoto, they run into reinforcements under the command of Niwa Nagahide, who has crossed over from Sakai with a small fleet of ships at Hideyoshi's request for assistance. Joining forces, they now

Opposite page: Shibata Katsuie

英雄三十六歌撰
柴田勝家

turn back towards Mount Shizugatake and jointly attack Morimasa's troops, forcing them to retreat to the abandoned fortress atop Mount Ooiwa.

By now Hideyoshi, who is still held up at Ōgaki Castle, has received word that Katsuie has gone on the offensive. And now he sets out to repeat what he did in the wake of Nobunaga's assassination when he moved his army from Takamatsu to Yamasaki—covering some 130 miles—in a matter of days. It is already noon, and the first thing he does is to send ahead messengers with orders to local village headmen to have people place torches along the length of the route and light them when his army will be passing through. Parcels of food and drink, too, are to be prepared and given to those who are hungry.

Departing from Ōgaki Castle at two o'clock in the afternoon, June 10, Hideyoshi's army arrives at Nagahama at seven o'clock that evening—they have covered the thirty-five-mile stretch in just five hours. That night his men are allowed to rest from their exhausting feat, but the next day they join the remaining forces holding out at their respective fortresses and launch a massive counter-attack on Morimasa's men atop Mount Ooiwa.

It is at this crucial juncture that Maeda Toshiie, who has stationed five thousand men atop Mount Shige, just north of Lake Yogo, orders his men to

Hideyoshi's warriors launch their conter-attack

withdraw and return to his headquarters of Fuchū in Echizen. Toshiie only reluctantly joined Katsuie. In the wake of Nobunaga's death, he had been stationed up north, fighting alongside Katsuie's forces to subdue the rebellious Uesugi Kagekatsu in the siege of Uozu Castle. By then he had already had a long career in Katsuie's service, which he had entered as a *yoriki* or chief of police. When the rift between Hideyoshi and Katsuie's appeared, he naturally chose the side of Katsuie, a chieftain who like him was based in Echizen. Yet he is on equally good terms with Hideyoshi and has been part of a failed initiative to restore relations between the two rivals.

Toshiie's retreat has a devastating effect on the morale of the other warriors. Aware that their rear is no longer protected, Morimasa's men are the

Katō Kiyomasa grapples with Masaji Masakuni

first to waver, especially when Masaji Masakuni, the commander who hatched the plan for the successful assault, falls in battle. He does so at the hands of Katō Kiyomasa, Hideyoshi's brilliant general, who leads the counter-attack.

Sakuma Morimasa seeks to hold out, but his men fail him. They have spent two days giving their all, but now they begin to lose heart and retreat the way they have come, toward Katsuie's troops farther north. This, in turn, causes Katsuie's forces to lose heart too. They too begin to move back along the Hokkoku Kaidō, and before long the whole of Katsuie's army is fleeing northwards, across the border into Echizen and to the safety of Kitanoshō Castle.

It is clear that Toshiie is afraid of Hideyoshi, for no sooner has he returned to his headquarters of Fuchū Castle than he also sues for peace. Hideyoshi accepts, but only on the condition that Toshiie will lead the vanguard in an attack against Katsuie's power base of Kitanoshō Castle, ten miles north of Fuchū Castle. He does so reluctantly, but he does so nevertheless.

Afterward, in a long letter to the western warlord Kobayakawa Takakage, a former ally of the Mōri with whom he has meanwhile established friendly ties, Hideyoshi describes Katsuie's last moments as his men storm the castle:

> On April 24 [June 14], at the hour of the Tiger [4 o'clock in the morning] we reached the castle itself and by noon we entered and killed all inside. Some two hundred of Katsuie's men were holding out inside the castle tower, and since it was so cramped inside, to storm the tower in full force would yield too many wounded and dead. And so we selected a number of men armed with swords and lances to cut and thrust their way inside. Being a man of great valor, Katsuie threw them back up to seven times, but at length, he had to give way. He climbed to the castle's ninth store, from where he addressed his men, shouting, 'Look on and see how one should cut one's belly.' At this, his retainers wept in the sleeves of their armor, and everyone grew silent as Katsuie proceeded to cut down his wife and children and

Kiyomasa and his men collect their trophies in the wake of the battle

Opposite page: Katsuie and Oichi prepare for the inevitable end

commit ritual suicide. He did so by formally cutting a cross in his belly and calling on his retainer Nakamura Bunkasai to act as *kaishaku*. And some eighty of his retainers followed suit. Then Bunkasai set fire to a charge of gunpowder he had prepared in advance. And thus the castle tower and all of Katsuie's clan were utterly destroyed.

Like her former husband, Nagamasa, Katsuie urges his wife to make her escape. But Oichi no Kata refuses. Once before she has abandoned her husband for the sake of her infant children. This time she chooses to join her husband in death. But before she does so, she sends her three daughters into the arms of her enemy, Hideyoshi, on the condition that they will be spared.

Sakuma Morimasa, too, achieves immortality. Having fled across the border into Echizen he is, like Mitsuhide, caught by a gang of armed peasants seeking reward for capturing *ochimusha*. Yet he manages to persuade them to spare his life and bring him to Hideyoshi, so he can argue his case to the vic-

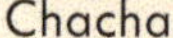

Chacha

Hatsu

Eyo

As he had done during the siege of Odani Castle, Hideyoshi takes good care of Oichi no Kata's daughters. The eldest, Chacha, becomes one of his concubines and goes on to give him his only natural son, Hideyori. The second, Hatsu, is married off to Kyōgoku Takatsugu, the master of Ōtsu Castle in Ōmi. The youngest, Eyo, however, will go farthest, for she becomes the wife of the second *Shōgun*, Tokugawa Hidetada, and the mother of the third Shogun, Iemitsu.

柴田修理進勝家
小谷の方
哥麿筆

Sakuma Morimasa surrenders himself to Hideyoshi

tor in person. They do so but fail to reap their reward from Hideyoshi, who has them summarily executed. Morimasa, however, he treats with leniency, offering him the province of Higo if he will help him subdue the island of Kyushu. But, according to the *Kawasumi taikōki*, Morimasa declines. 'Were you to let me live, I would certainly kill you if I would ever see you. I would rather have you put me to death.' And thus Hideyoshi relents, offering him a warrior's death by allowing him to commit ritual suicide. But again Morimasa declines, insisting he should be put to death like a general of a defeated army. 'I'd prefer you to load me on a cart and drive me around the capital from the intersection of Ichijō to show high and low alike how you have me in fetters. In that way, your name will resound throughout the realm.' And thus it happens. Afterward, he is brought to Uji, where he is beheaded like a defeated general. He is only thirty years old.

KOMAKI & NAGAKUTE

Ieyasu, meanwhile, has not been sitting on his laurels either. From the day he has returned to Hamamatsu Castle in the wake of the Honnō Rebellion, news of unrest has been pouring in from all corners of his sphere of influence. Only a few months have passed since he and Nobunaga vanquished Takeda Katsuyori. They have left the governance of the region in the hands of Takigawa Kazumasu. But as soon as word of Nobunaga's death has spread, rebellions have started in Kai and Shinano. At the same time, the Uesugi are making inroads into Kai from Echigo, while the Hōjō are doing the same in Musashi and Kōzuke. Kazumasu does his best to control the situation, but already powerful chieftains on whom he relies are abandoning their castles and fleeing westward.

Ieyasu sends Sakai Tadatsugu into Shinano to assist Kazumasu there, while he himself leads his army into Kai along the Nakamichi Highroad. Arriving in Kōfu on July 28, he first sets up headquarters at the Sontai-ji, a temple founded in 1521 by Takeda Nobutora. There he spends the next weeks conducting his campaign to bring the region back under his control, all the while he communicates his actions in great detail to Hideyoshi, who approves his actions. Needless to say, Ieyasu isn't acting on behalf of himself but—like Hideyoshi—in the name of Oda Nobunaga. But in truth these two powerful men are now positioning themselves to succeed their former lord: Hideyoshi

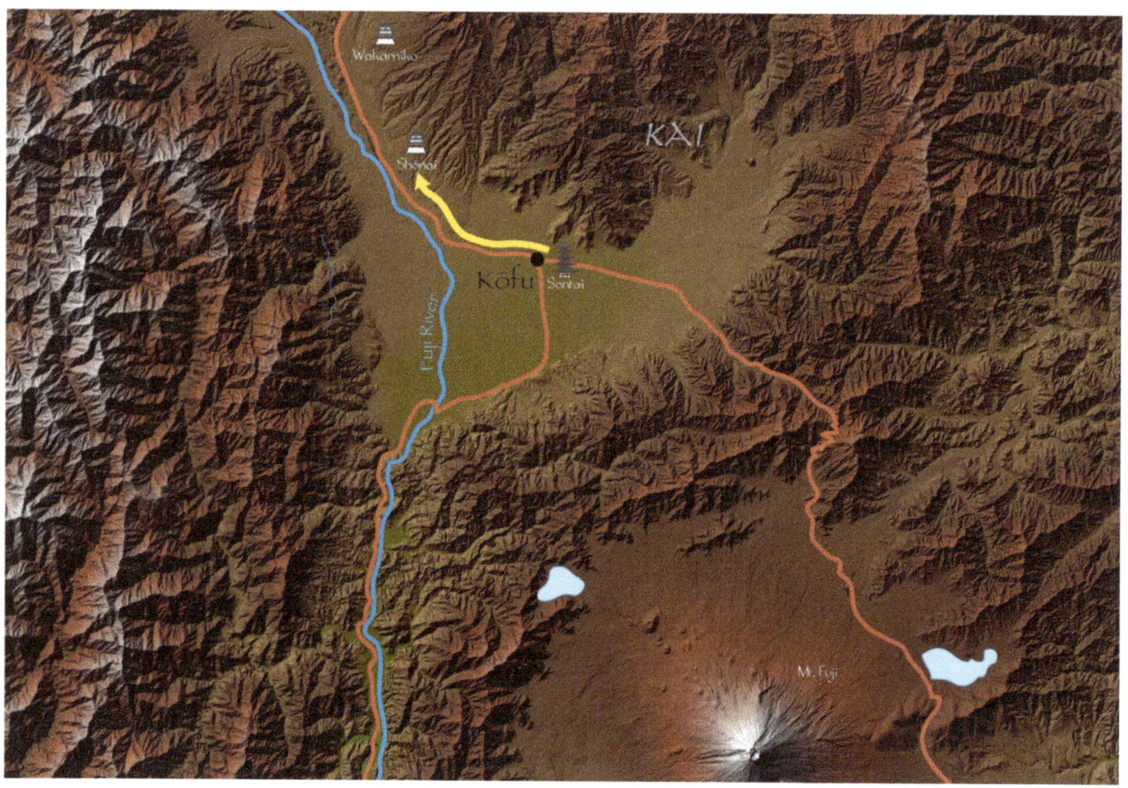

by defeating Mitsuhide at Yamasaki and Katsuie at Shizugatake; Ieyasu by gaining control of Kai and Shinano. For a moment it looks like Ieyasu might fail when Hōjō Ujiteru and some fifty thousand warriors take up positions at Wakamiko Castle, just fifteen miles north of Kōfu. To face off the threat Ieyasu moves his headquarters to Shinpu Castle, situated halfway. But the Hōjō have no stomach to fight him. After a minor victory by one of Ieyasu's vassals at a place called Kurokoma, the two sides make peace, leaving the Hōjō to pick up only Kōzuke, while Ieyasu is able to add Kai and Shinano to his provinces of Mikawa, Tōtōmi, and Suruga.

Thus the stage is set for Ieyasu and Hideyoshi to test each other's strength. It is a member of the Oda clan, the equally ambitious Nobukatsu, who this time proves to be the catalyst. Following Katsuie's demise, Nobukatsu lays siege to Gifu Castle, where his younger brother, Nobukata, is still holding out. Deprived of an ally, Nobukata realizes his situation is hopeless and lets

Opposite page: Takigawa Kazumasu, the man put in control of Kai and Shinano

太平記英勇傳
滝川左近一益
山全亭有人記
一惠齋芳幾筆
三十五

himself be persuaded to surrender. He is taken to the Noma Daibō Temple in Owari where, on June 21, 1583, he is forced to commit *seppuku*. All this has been done on the prompting of his brother Nobukatsu, who, as the sole guardian of Nobunaga's infant heir, believes he can now lord it over Nobunaga's former general, Hideyoshi. In this, of course, he is soon disappointed. The year is hardly out when he and Hideyoshi fall out as they meet at Sakamoto to discuss the future of the realm. Returning to his headquarters of Nagashima Castle, Nobukatsu now turns to Ieyasu, who reciprocates his advances by agreeing to an alliance. To counter the threat, Hideyoshi seeks to win the support of three of Nobukasu's retainers. In response, Nobukatsu sentences the three men to death and declares war on Hideyoshi.

To Ieyasu, his new alliance is merely one of convenience, nothing near his pact with Nobukatsu's father, who outstripped all his sons. Now Ieyasu is the stronger partner in the Oda-Tokugawa alliance. There is no comparison really; his Mikawa warriors belong to the best in the realm, and with his

Inuyama Castle, the stronghold captured by Ikeda Tsuneoki

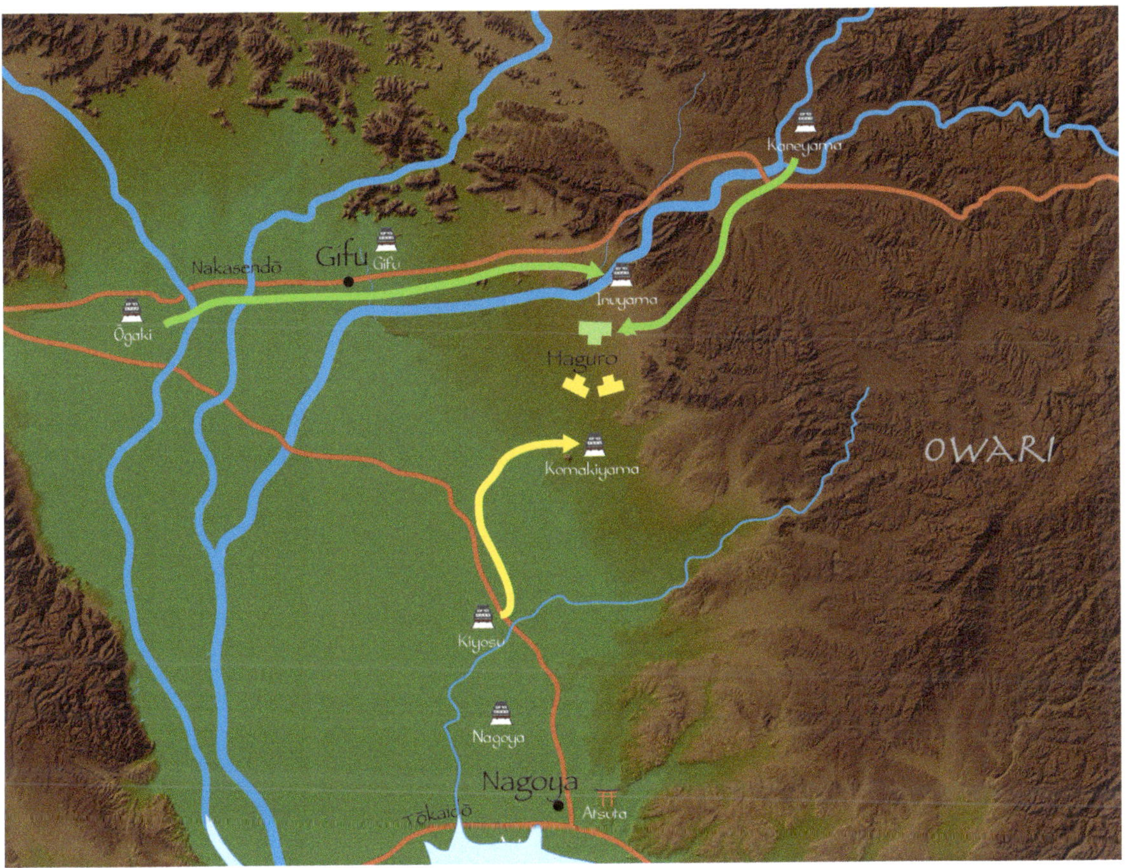

recent acquisition of Kai and Shinano he has also recruited many former Takeda vassals, all men whose military skill has been honed under the legendary Shingen. Among them is a certain Obata Kagenori, the man who has spent the better part of his life compiling the *Kōyō gunkan*, the lengthy compendium on the Takeda clan's art of military strategy, and it is in this revolutionary work in which Ieyasu makes his generals immerse themselves on their time away from the battlefield. To further strengthen his position, he marries one of his daughters off to Hōjō Ujinao, thus securing his rear for the moment he will have to deal with Hideyoshi's attack from the west—a moment he now knows will inevitably come.

That moment comes in the spring of 1584 when on 23 April, Ikeda Tsuneoki, the master of Ōgaki Castle and a former Nobunaga vassal, declares

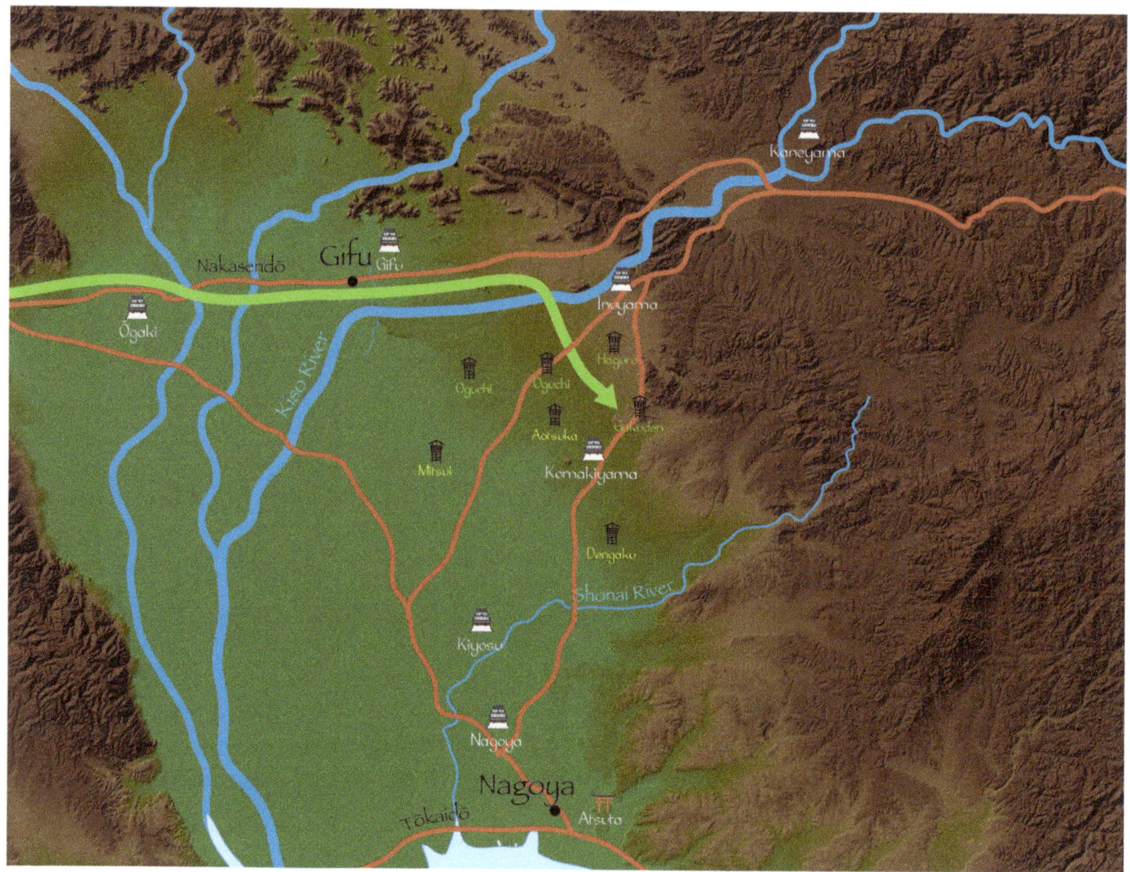

himself for Hideyoshi and occupies Inuyama Castle. Ieyasu, who is just then at Kiyosu Castle, is still somewhat taken by surprise, but immediately lays siege to Komakiyama Castle, situated just seven miles south of Inuyama. This, in turn, leads Mori Nagayoshi, another former Oda vassal and Tsuneoki's son-in-law, to equally declare himself for Hideyoshi. Not wanting to be outdone, he sets out from his headquarters of Kaneyama Castle, some fifteen miles upstream along the Kiso River from Inuyama, and takes up position at Haguro with some five thousand of his men, thus forming the vanguard to his father-in-law's troops at Inuyama Castle. Ieyasu, who has meanwhile taken Komakiyama Castle, counters by dispatching two of his best generals, Matsudaira Ietada and Sakai Tadatsugu, who take up position opposite Nagayoshi's forces with another five thousand.

The next day, April 27, Tadatsuge launches a withering assault on Nagayoshi's front. For a moment it seems Nagayoshi's men will stand their ground, but when they are fired upon by a unit of Ietada's musketeers they begin to retreat. Ietada, who has kept behind most of his men thus far, now sends them round to try and attack the enemy from the rear, and what had begun as an orderly retreat soon turns into a disorderly flight. At the end of the day, some three hundred Mori men have lost their lives at Haguro.

On the first of May, increasingly worried by the unfortunate turn events are taking, Hideyoshi departs from Osaka Castle at the head of thirty thousand troops. He arrives at Inuyama six days later and sets up camp at Gakuden, just south of Haguro. By now, both camps have entrenched themselves by erecting a large number of fortresses and fortifications; what at first had seemed like a conflict that would be decided by a quick and decisive fight has developed into something that might drag on for weeks and months.

It is with a view to breaking this apparent stalemate—and to expiate his son-in-law's role in creating it—that, on May 13, Ikeda Tsuneoki visits Hideyoshi at Gakuden and proposes to lead a large force across the border into Mikawa and menace Ieyasu's homeland by setting fire to villages and generally terrorizing the population. This, he argues, will surely force Ieyasu

Honda Tadakatsu and Sakai Tadatsugu hold Komakiyama Castle

to come to his people's aid and abandon his positions in Owari. The next day he again visits Hideyoshi, who has by now been won over by Tsuneoki's plan. And thus, on May 15, Tsuneoki sets out from Inuyama with some six thousand men and heads for Mikawa. His army is supported by three flying columns: three thousand men under Mori Nagayoshi; another three thousand under Hori Hidemasa; and eight thousand under Hideyoshi's nephew, the sixteen-year-old Hidetsugu.

Despite their nocturnal departure Tsuneoki's troops are soon spotted by Ieyasu's scouts, who report that a flying column of the enemy force led by Hidetsugu has been seen encamped at Shinogi, on the northern bank of the Shonai River. On the evening of May 17, Ieyasu responds by sending a spearhead army of four thousand men under the command of his uncle, Mizuno

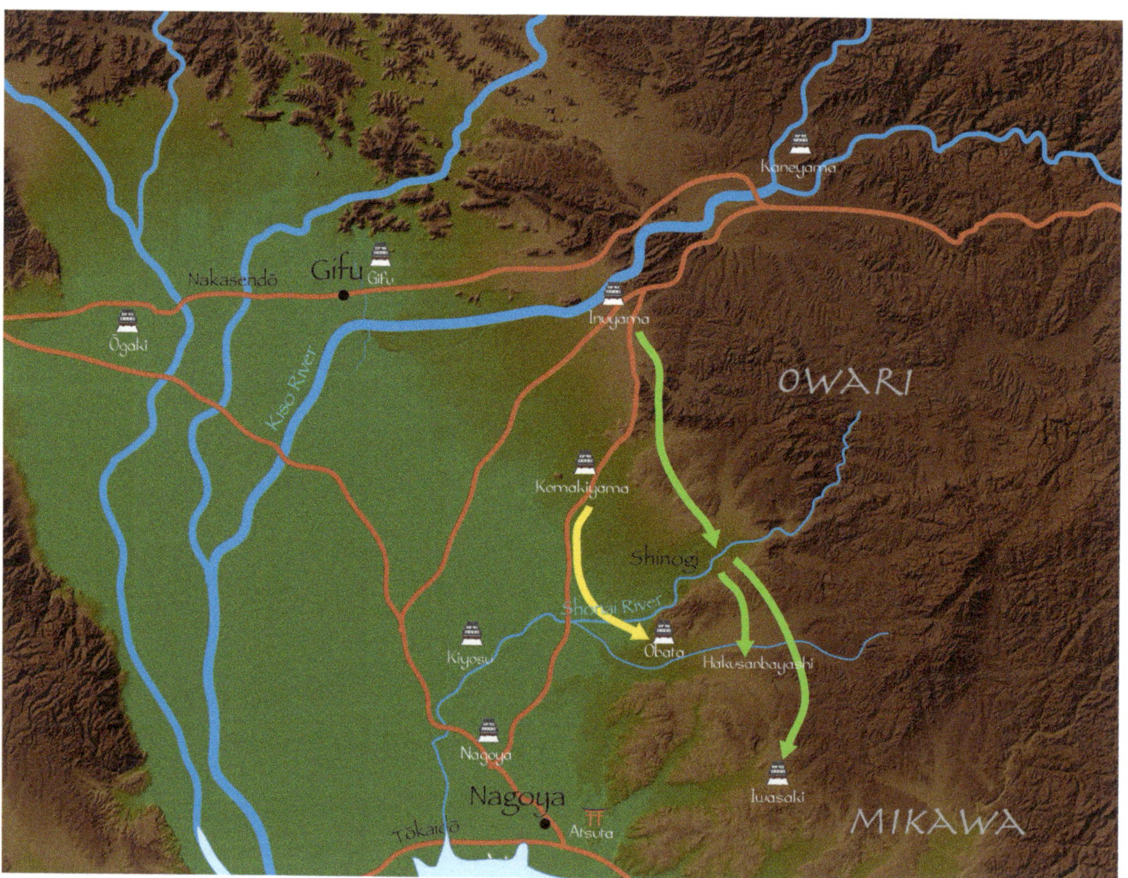

Sakakibara Yasumasa strikes Hidetsugu's forces in the flank

Tadashige, across the Shonai River to occupy Obata Castle. Then he instructs Honda Tadakatsu and Sakai Tadatsugu to hold Komakiyama Castle at all costs.

A few hours later he and Nobukatsu depart with the rest of his force, arriving at Obata Castle at midnight. At dawn the next morning Hidetsugu crosses the Yada River. But no sooner have he and his men crossed the river's shallow waters than he orders his men to halt near Hakusanbayashi for another rest. By then Ieyasu has set his trap. Bringing his troops round in a circular movement, Mizuno Tadashige launches a full-scale attack on Hidetsugu's army from the south, while Sakakibara Yasumasa (like Honda Tadakatsu one of Ieyasu's *hatamoto*) strikes them in the flank. The attack comes as such an utter surprise to the complacent Hidetsugu that he loses his horse in the melee. Yet instead of making a brave stand, the youth grabs the steed of one of his retainers to make his escape, and it is only through the valiant sacrifice of his retainers that he is able to do so.

Things aren't faring much better for Tsuneoki and his men. Having reached the vicinity of Iwasaki Castle at dawn, May 18, they set fire to a number of nearby fortifications. Their aim is to capture Iwasaki Castle, but spotting the fires, its master, Niwa Ujishige launches a fierce attack on Tsuneoki's encampment, even though he only has a few hundred men. Driven

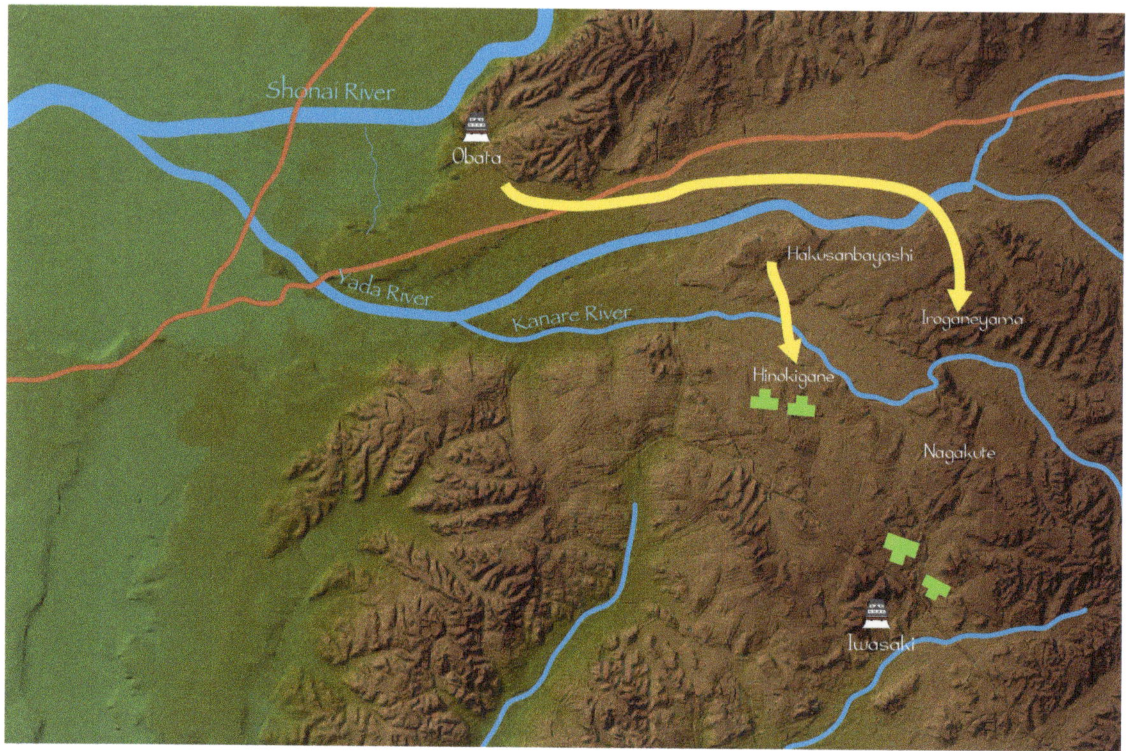

back into his castle he manages to repulse Tsuneoki's men up to three times. But when the latter are reinforced by a large unit of Mori musketeers, Ujishige loses his life. He is only fifteen years old, a year younger than Hideyoshi's cowardly nephew. Yet his death isn't in vain. The news of his selfless example soon reaches the ears of Sakakibara Yasumasa, who is deeply touched by the 'splendid end of Master Ujishige and his men,' and vows he will 'slay the enemy in the coming battle.' Hearing this, Ujishige's brother, who has joined Ieyasu and on whose behalf he has stayed behind at Iwasaki Castle, thanks Yasumasa for his kind words, and echoes his sentiments.

Hearing of Hidetsugu's defeat, Hori Hidemasa, who is roughly halfway to Iwasaki, and keenly aware of the danger of having his retreat cut off, immediately orders his men to turn back. They catch up with the remnants of Hidetsugu's army and together they set up camp at Hinokigane, on the southern bank of the Kanare River. Here too they are attacked by Yasumasa's men, who are still drunk on their earlier victory over their enemy, but Hidemasa manages to drive then back to the Kanare River, killing several hundred of them. With no further obstacles in his way, Hidemasa orders his men to move southward, so as to join the main army ay Iwasaki Castle.

Meanwhile, Ieyasu and Nobukatsu have led the bulk of their army eastward, from Obata Castle to Irogane-*yama*, a shallow hill, where, just after four o'clock in the morning, he sets up his headquarters. It is there that he learns of Yasumasa's victory and defeat that morning, and that Hidemasa is moving towards Iwasaki. He immediately orders his men to move farther southward and take up positions at Fujigane, so as to drive a wedge between Hidemasa and Iwasaki Castle. He needn't have worried; the sight of Ieyasu's banner atop Irogane-*yama* alone is enough for Hidemasa to retreat, back across the Kanare River. This leaves Ikeda Tsuneoki and Mori Nagayoshi in the lurch. They are in possession of Iwasaki Castle, but their plan to menace

The hotly contested stronghold of Iwasaki Castle

The two armies clash at Nagakute

Ieyasu's homelands has come to nothing; they are cut off and their only hope lies in turning back and face Ieyasu out in the open.

By the time the Ikeda and Mori armies take up positions, Ieyasu has moved his three thousand and three hundred men forward, to a place known as Nagakute by locals. Just towards the east from them are another three thousand under the command of Ii Naomasa, and the same number under Oda Nobukatsu. Facing the latter are four thousand men under Tsuneoki's two sons, while Mori's men face those of Ieyasu. Tsuneoki himself has positioned himself farther to the rear with another two thousand.

For a while, the two armies stare each other down, but then, at ten o'-clock in the morning, May 18, 1584, the two armies clash. For the next two hours, each struggles to gain the advantage. But at noon, having driven his attack home until he is almost within reach of Ieyasu's headquarters, Mori Nagayoshi is struck in the head by a bullet from an Ii sniper. Sensing the Mori men are faltering without their general, the whole of Ieyasu's army now sweeps round to fall on Tsuneoki's reserve. One of them, a lancer by the name of Nagai Denpachirō, spots Tsuneoki sitting on a camp stool. Rushing up to him he runs him through with his yari and takes his head. It is now almost one o'clock. Then, shortly after his father, Tsuneoki's eldest son, Motosuke, too is killed. The battle has run its course.

Separated from the theatre of battle by some twenty miles, Hideyoshi finds himself in a vexing time warp, unable to catch up with events. Hearing of his nephew's dismal performance at Hakusanbayashi, he has rushed his army southward, but on the way, they are harassed by a small force under the command of Honda Tadakatsu. They haven't even reached the banks of the Shonai River when Hideyoshi hears the news that Ieyasu is safely back at Obata Castle. By now dusk has set in and thus he decides to postpone his attack till the next morning. But that nigh Ieyasu steals himself away and moves back to Komakiyama Castle. This news too reaches Hideyoshi hours later, so that he finally withdraws his forces back to Rakuden. He has been utterly outwitted by his opponent.

Hideyoshi, of course, is thoroughly vexed by his elusive enemy, especially when the latter refuses to be cajoled into leaving the safety of Komakiyama Castle and face him in the field. And thus he spends the next few months trying to weaken Ieyasu's support in the region. On June 12, he lays siege to Kaganoi, Oku, and Takegahana Castle. Missives are sent from all three strongholds to Ieyasu and Nobukatsu for relief, but he still refuses to budge, advising them instead to surrender. This they refuse to do, even though they face a superior force led by a superior commander.

Honda Tadakatsu observes Hideyoshi's retreat

Kaganoi Castle is the first to fall after Hideyoshi's men spend two days setting fire to most of its environs. And though the womenfolk and common soldiers are spared, all its officers are put to death. Oku Castle follows next. Takegahana Castle is the only one to hold out. And thus Hideyoshi resorts to the same method by which he has reduced Takamatsu Castle. Over the next few weeks, he puts his men and locals to work to build a ten feet high and two-mile-long, crescent-shaped dam around the castle and across the two rivers in which confluence it sits. His tactic soon takes effect. The rainy

Takegahana Castle (encircled), sitting in the confluence of two rivers

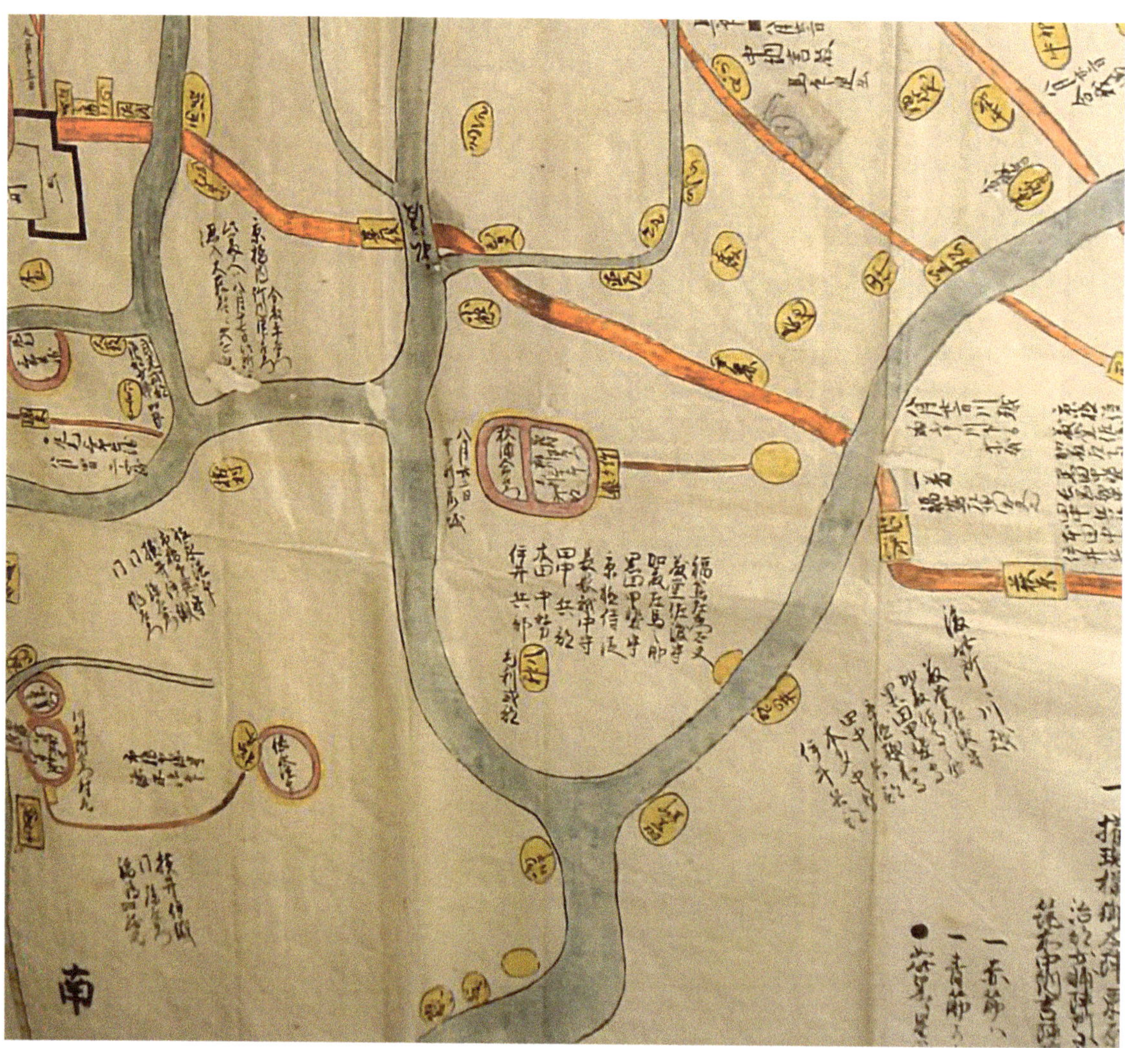

The siege of Takegahana Castle

season has meanwhile begun and before long all but the inner citadel is several feet deep in water. Its garrison makes due by building ramparts to stay dry, while inside the main keep the womenfolk are terrorized by a host of vermin seeking refuge on higher ground.

For almost a month those within the castle manage to keep their feet dry. During that time a relief part under the command of Honda Tadakatsu tries to reach the castle, but they too are cornered by Hideyoshi's army and forced to retreat. At length, realizing nothing will draw his opponent into an open fight, Hideyoshi relents and promises to spare the lives of all inside on the condition they surrender. On June 7, the castle is relinquished. Satisfied he has saved face, Hideyoshi orders his army to retreat and one month later, on August 4, he returns to Osaka Castle.

Hideyoshi (left) and Ieyasu have reached a truce

The next few months see some desultory fighting throughout the region, but that winter, on December 13, Hideyoshi and Nobukatsu reach a settlement in which half of Iga and Ise are ceded to Hideyoshi. Without a just cause (*taigi meibun*) to challenge Hideyoshi, Ieyasu too relents and returns to Hamamatsu Castle. There he is visited by one of Hideyoshi's envoys, who offers him a peace settlement. As insurance, he is required to provide a hostage. Ieyasu accepts, and shortly afterward, his second son, Ogimaru (Yuki Hideyasu) is sent to Osaka Castle to become one of Hideyoshi's adopted sons—again Ieyasu has offered up a son for the sake of peace, though this time the boy is allowed to live.

SEKIGAHARA

In the summer of 1598, feeling his strength ebbing and realizing his end is drawing near, Hideyoshi calls into life the institutions that will ensure he is succeeded by his infant son, Hideyori. Drawing on the organs of state of the Muromachi *Bakufu* that have survived Nobunaga's rule, he forms two councils of five men each. The one with most authority is the *Go-Tairō*, the Council of (five) Regents. Its members are Tokugawa Ieyasu, Maeda Toshiie, Mōri Terumoto, Uesugi Kagekatsu, and Ukita Hideie. These men, his most trusted vassals, are to safeguard continued Toyotomi rule. The second organ of state is that of the *Go-Bugyō*, the Council of (five) Commissioners. Its members are Ishida Mitsunari, Asano Nagamasa, Maeda Geni, Mashita Nagamori, and Natsuka Masaie. The *bugyō* are directly responsible to the *tairō* and in charge of the day-to-day administrative affairs of government. Satisfied that he has done all he can to secure his son's succession, on September 5, Hideyoshi once again calls Ieyasu to his bedside and makes him swear once more that he will obey his every injunction. Two weeks later the *Taikō-sama* is dead and the future of his heir in the hands of Ieyasu and the other *tairō*.

Ieyasu dutifully complies with all of Hideyoshi's wishes, as do all the other warlords—to do otherwise is to court certain disaster. And, at least for the time being, Ieyasu is content with the arrangement. The death one year later of Maeda Toshiie, the new lord of Osaka Castle, makes him the most pow-

Osaka Castle, with in the foreground the western wing

erful warlord among the five tairō, a position that he underscores with characteristic decisiveness when, on Toshiie's death, he moves into the western wing of the vacated castle and is recognized by the other *tairō* as the *Tenka-dono*, the "lord of the realm."

Ieyasu's supremacy, however, is not undisputed. Contrary to Hideyoshi's intentions, there is little unity among the *tairō* and *bugyō*. Soon after his death, the two councils begin to fall apart into two rival factions, one coalescing around Ieyasu, the other around the western warlord Ishida Mitsunari. The real power the factions exercise is not expressed in the official position their members occupy, but in the extent of the territories they and their adherents control, as this is the basis for the military might each faction can bring to the fore. To extend the power of his faction and consolidate his position, Ieyasu falls back on the age-old method of intermarriage, binding to him and his adherents those warlords who can tip the balance of power in his favor.

Meanwhile, Ieyasu watches with Argus eyes how Mitsunari furtively positions himself for a major confrontation, forging secret alliances with other western warlords without giving Ieyasu any direct cause to accuse him of treachery. What Ieyasu needs is a ploy, an excuse by which to draw the shrewd and wily Mitsunari from his den and expose his treachery to the other *tairō*, thus creating for himself a *taigi meibun*, a just cause to deal with Mitsunari.

That opportunity presents itself in the spring of 1600 when reports begin to reach Osaka Castle that one of Ieyasu's fellow *tairō*, the northern warlord Uesugi Kagekatsu, is reinforcing his positions in the province of Aizu. He has issued secret orders to his vassals to prepare their strongholds for war and has even begun on the construction of a new stronghold, Kōzashi Castle, at the center of the Aizu Basin. Like Kenshin, Kagekatsu has always been an obstacle to the drive towards centralized control, but with his power base far removed from the center of power and only half the talent of his adoptive father, he has never posed a serious threat to Ieyasu's designs. Now, for a change, he comes in handy by providing Ieyasu with the perfect pretext to act. Already Ieyasu has repeatedly summoned Kagekatsu to come down to Osaka Castle and explain his conduct. As anticipated, the belligerent warlord blatantly ignores the summons and continues to build up his forces around his headquarters of Aizu Wakamatsu Castle.

A joint letter by the *gotairō*, with Ieyasu's signature at the center

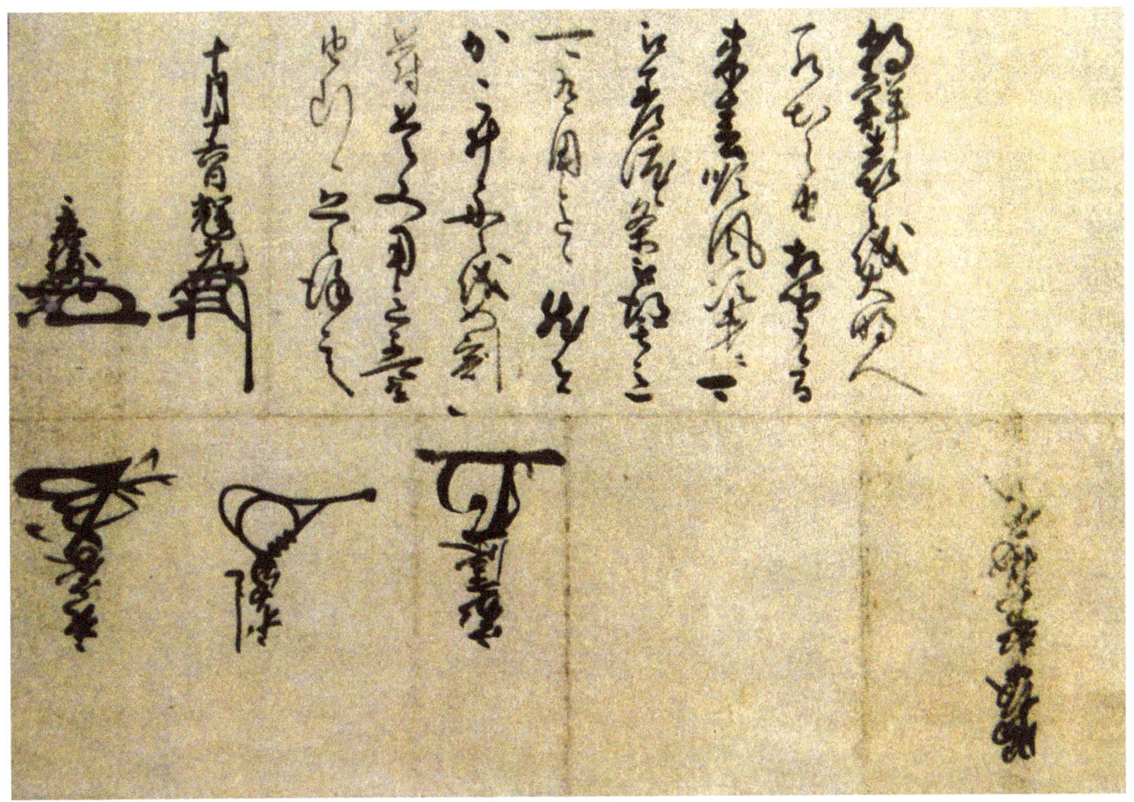

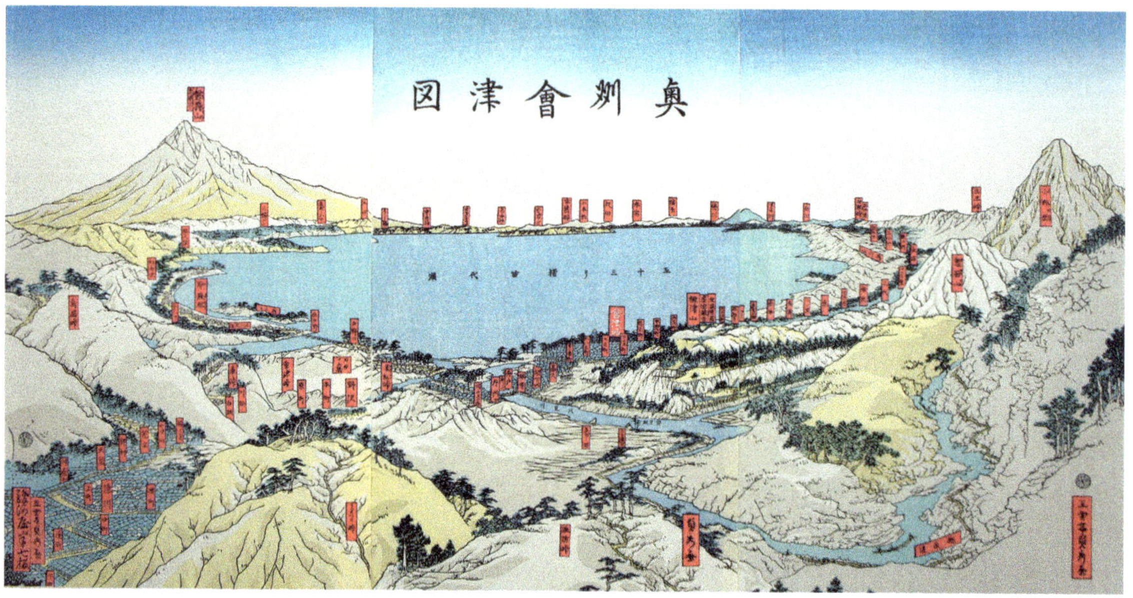

The Castle town of Aizu Wakamatsu, on the shore of Lake Inawashro

And thus, early in July, Ieyasu decides to travel up to Edo Castle, from where he intends to conduct a campaign to quell the rebellious warlord and—more importantly—to await the first signs of Mitsunari's revolt. First, however, he calls at Fushimi Castle, for it is there that he expects Mitsunari and his fellow conspirators to strike first. To stall Mitsunari's advance, he leaves Torii Mototada and some fifteen hundred of his best warriors in charge of the castle's defense. It is far too small a force to withstand a sustained assault, but sufficient to keep Mitsunari tied down long enough for Ieyasu to take care of Kagekatsu. He does not intend to be pinned down in the north with his rear vulnerable to attack. Yet he knows that it is that very assumption that will lead Mitsunari to show his colors. It is all he requires.

On August 29, Ieyasu departs from Edo and sets out northward, towards Oyama, in Shimotsuke, a three day's journey from Wakamatsu Castle. Reaching the place on September 1, he sets up camp and orders all the warlords who have joined him on his northern expedition to assemble for a war council the next day. By now he has his taigi meibun: Three days earlier, Mōri Terumoto has entered Osaka Castle and raised the Toyotomi banner. Mitsunari himself is still holding up at his headquarters of Sawayama Castle, on the easter shore of Lake Biwa, but it is only a matter of time now before he too will move. The next day, September 2, Ieyasu and his allies set out the strategy by which he intends to counter Mitsunari's challenge. A number of the assembled warlords are told to return home to their domains and raise yet more troops. Most, however, are ordered to lead their troops down the Tōkaidō to Kiyosu Castle, just west of Nagoya. There they are to await the arrival of the others, as well as Ieyasu's son, Hidetada, who will lead the rest of Ieyasu's troops down the Nakasendō.

By September 12, Ieyasu is back in Edo. Following his war council at Oyama, he has ordered his Kantō allies to keep Kagekatsu in check so he can ready himself for the final confrontation with Ishida Mitsunari. Over the next weeks, from his headquarters of Edo Castle, Ieyasu continues to follow the movements of his enemies. Events are now unfolding in rapid succession. On his arrival, he learns that, on August 30, Ukita Hideie and a number of other western warlords have attacked Fushimi Castle. The castle falls after ten days of intense fighting in which Torii Mototada and all his men have lost their lives. Mitsunari too has moved. Setting out from Sawayama Castle on September 16, he has marched eastward along the Nakasendō, entering the small stronghold of Ōgaki Castle one day later without encountering any

Ieyasu and his retinue setting out from Edo Castle

resistance. It appears he wants to entrench himself in Mino, where he has won the support of Oda Hidenobu at Gifu Castle.

Ieyasu is not in the least perturbed by these tidings. He has given the two great armies that departed on the day following the council enough time to reach their destinations—something that is confirmed by the news, shortly after his arrival, that the force that has marched down the Tōkaidō has meanwhile reached the stronghold of Kiyosu according to plan. Ieyasu himself does not budge from Edo Castle. First, he wants to ascertain the loyalty of his commanders in the field—a loyalty that can only be expressed in military feats. Such is the purport of a message delivered to the gathered forces at Kiyosu on September 26, and it has the desired effect. Two days later, a contingent of five thousand men under the command of Ikeda Terumasa crosses the Kiso River upstream to attack Gifu Castle in force. They come under dense rifle fire from Oda Hidenobu's troops across the river, forcing them at

Ōgaki Castle

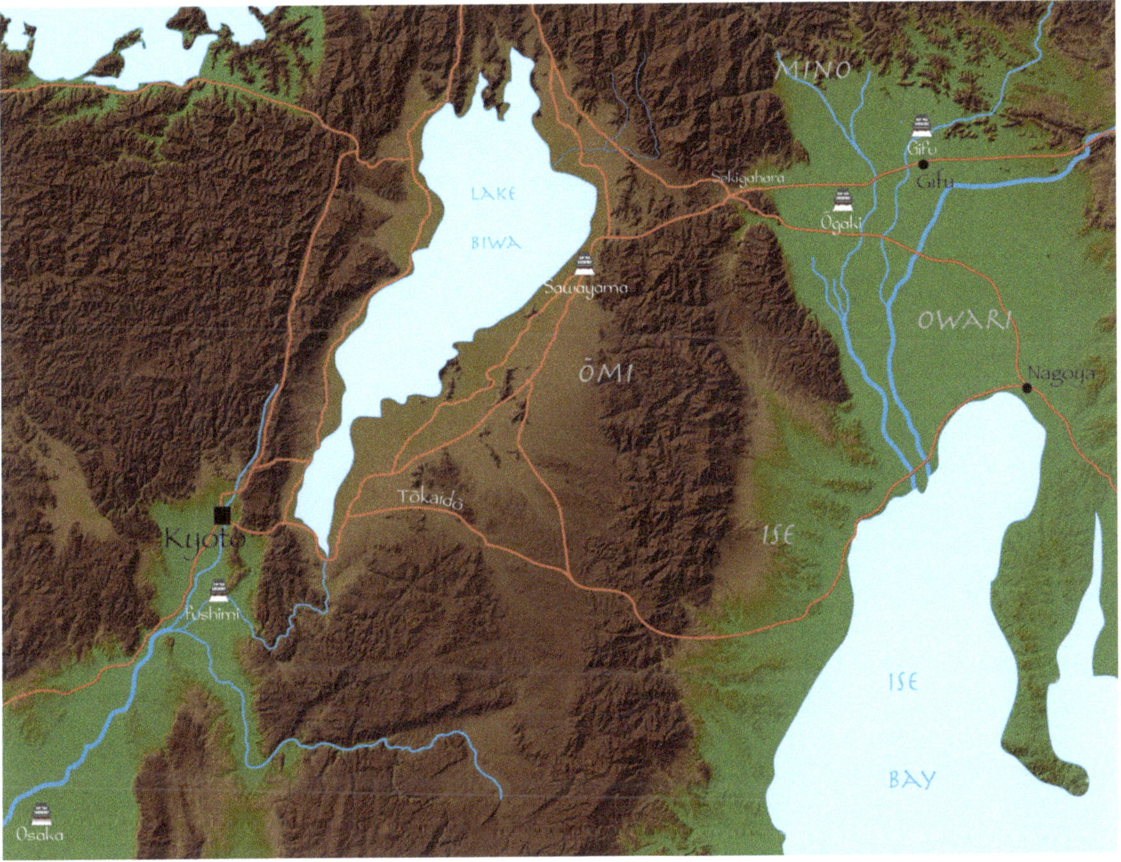

first to retreat. Then the scales tip. A second large eastern contingent, under the command of Fukushima Masanori, has crossed the river farther downstream by means of a fleet of small boats under the cover of night. At first, the Oda forces offer fierce resistance, but when they are threatened to be cut off, Hidenobu orders his men to retreat to the castle.

At early daybreak, on September 30 the Ikeda and Fukushima forces launch a massive attack on Gifu Castle. Within hours Masanori's men have forced one of the castle's gates and make their way into the castle's second bailey, the last line of defense protecting the keep where Oda Hidenobu and his family are holding out. Not much later Terumasa's men force their way into the castle's inner citadel, setting sections of it afire and hurling their banner into the castle's keep shouting 'today, we are the first to breach the

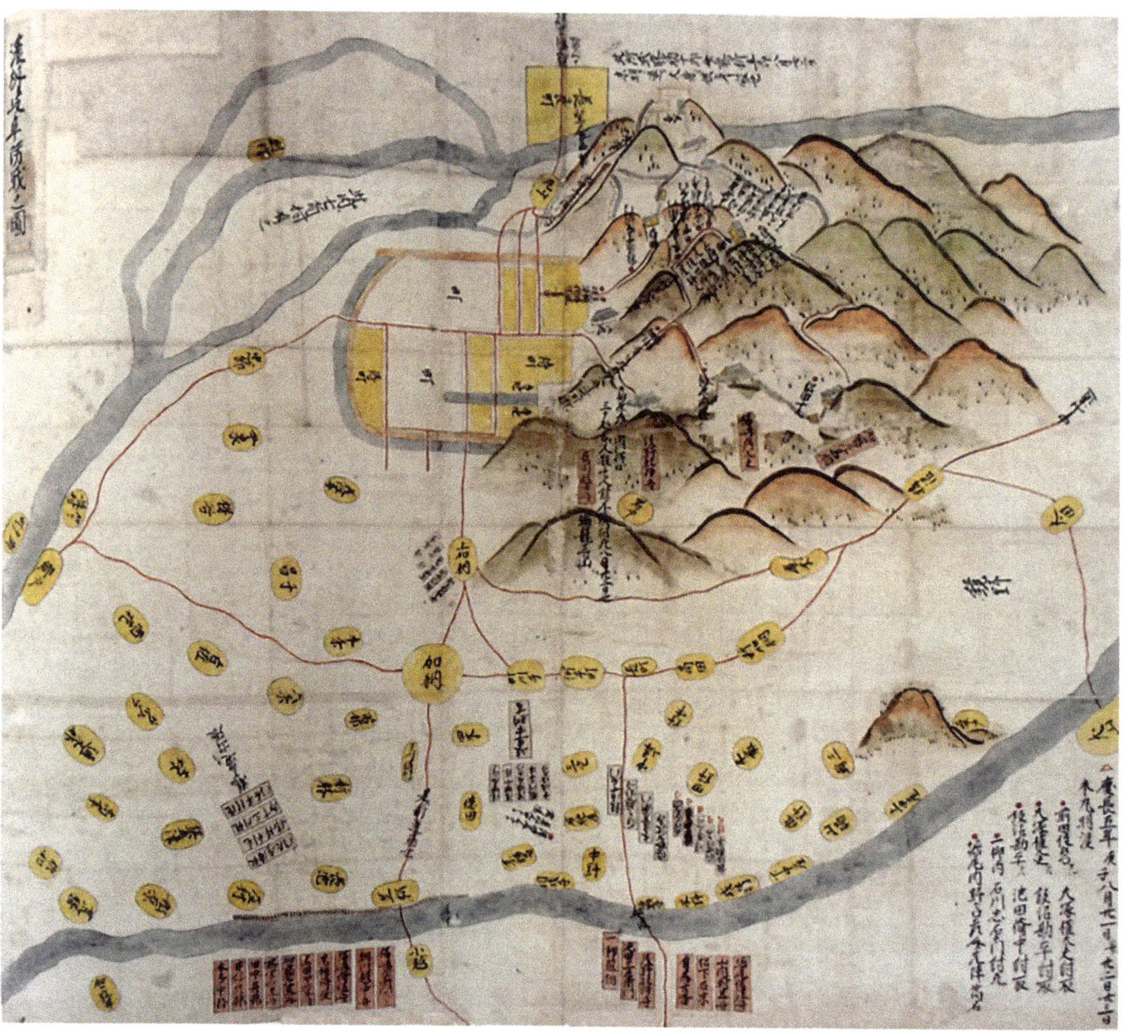

A map depicting the troop placements along the Kiso River, with the Tokugawa forces (in red) on the southern, and the Oda forces on the northern bank of the Kiso River

enemy's castle.' High up in the keep, Hidenobu, realizing his game is up, prepares to commit ritual suicide, when he is prevailed upon by his retainers to surrender and go into seclusion in Gifu's Entoku Temple. Hearing that Gifu Castle has fallen, the master of nearby Inuyama Castle too surrenders. All the commanders who have led their troops along the Tōkaidō now order their men to advance westward, toward Ōgaki Castle and Mitsunari's forces.

Mitsunari is stunned by the swiftness with which Ieyasu has turned the scales on him. Terumoto's forces have meanwhile invaded Ise Province. But in Mitsunari's plans, the castles of Ōgaki, Gifu, and Inuyama featured as a barrier to guard the gateway to the capital and the western provinces. It also seemed the perfect base from which to launch his intended strike against Ieyasu's home province of Mikawa and the Kantō beyond. Now those plans are rendered futile. Within only a few days the eastern army has captured two of his Mino strongholds. They now threaten to do the same with the castle where he and his allies have gathered. He panics and orders his troops to press forward, toward Gifu, to throw up a line of defense along the eastern shores of the Nagara River. The strategy backfires, and instead of throwing back the advancing eastern troops, Mitsunari is forced to withdraw to Ōgaki Castle at the cost of many casualties.

Seeing the huge force arrayed against him, Mitsunari now frantically begins to write letters to befriended warlords, luring them with the promise

Gifu Castle

of more territories and higher status. His efforts seem to bear fruit, for over the next few weeks one warlord after the other leads their troops into Mino and sets up camp in the vicinity of Ōgaki Castle. Among them are powerful men such as Ōtani Yoshitsugu, Ukita Hideie, Mōri Hidemoto, Kikkawa Hiroie, and Natsuka Masaie. Their combined forces comprise some thirty thousand men, bringing the total of the western forces close to eighty thousand, roughly twice the number of those arrayed against them. Even warlords of doubtful allegiance make their appearance, among them Kobayakawa Hideaki, who arrives with some eight thousand men in tow.

The eastern army has meanwhile pitched camp at the post station of Akasaka, some three miles northwest of Ōgaki. There are some twenty contingents in all, varying in number from a few hundred to several thousand. The largest is that of Kuroda Nagamasa, who has put well over five thousand warriors in the field. Another large contingent is that of Tsutsui Sadatsugu,

The old post town of Akasaka along the Nakasendō

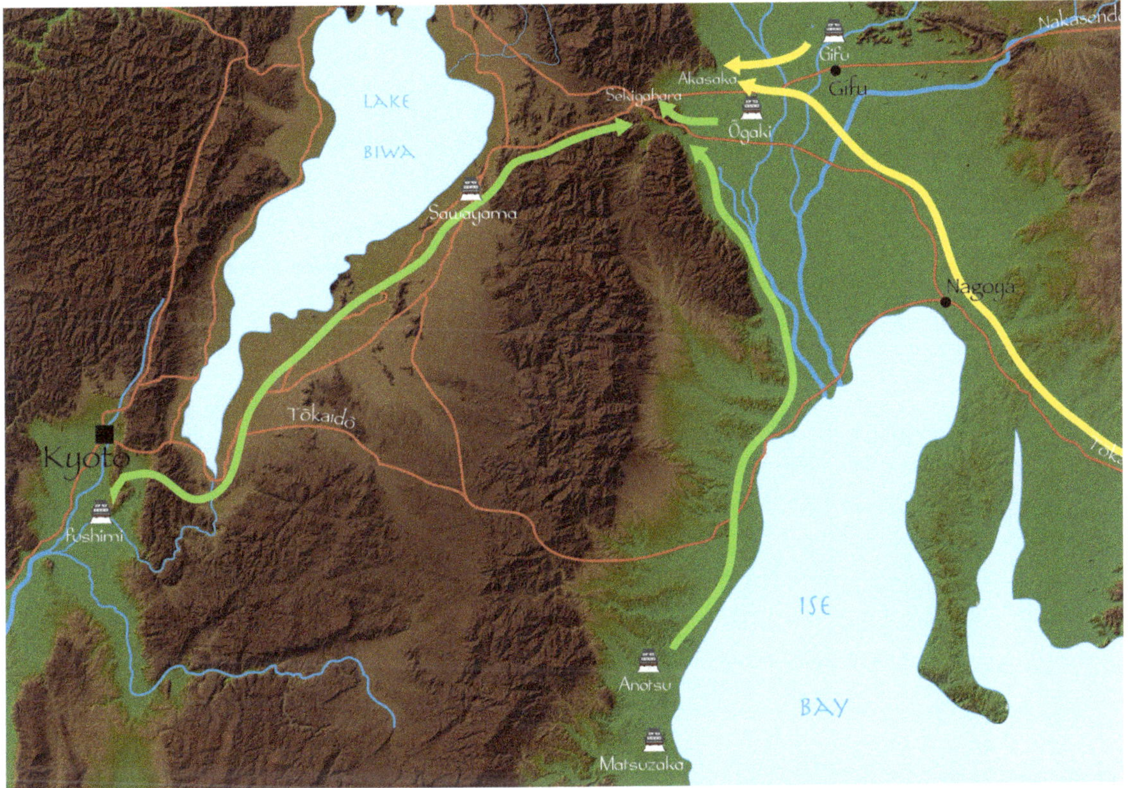

who has managed to raise close to three thousand men. They have departed from Ueno Castle toward the end of September and joined their allies shortly after the fall of Gifu and Inuyama Castles. There is no sign yet of Ieyasu, nor of his son Hidetada, who was to lead the second great force along the Nakasendō. And thus they impatiently await the arrival of Ieyasu, the great eastern commander who is to conduct the battle against Mitsunari and his western allies and thereby decide the fate of the nation.

Until the afternoon of October 20, the huge host of warriors, horses, carriers, and camp followers wait for the *Tenka-dono* to arrive. Ieyasu's arrival does not go unnoticed, neither to them nor to the enemy, for with him he has brought a contingent of thirty thousand troops, bringing the total number of men who have joined his side close to eighty thousand, almost the equivalent of those assembled under Ishida Mitsunari. His arrival is affirmed when his retainers erect the banners with the Tokugawa crest.

Its very name of Sekigahara, or Plains of the Barrier, hailed back to the old Fuwa barrier. That barrier had been erected at the end of the seventh century when, in the wake of the Jinshin Rebellion, Emperor Tenmu had ordered the erection of barriers along the Hokurikudō, the Tōkaidō, and the Nakasendō, the three main roads that connected the capital to the rest of the country. Though the Fuwa barrier itself did not last, throughout Japanese history the passage it had guarded had proven the place of the greatest strategic significance of the three. It had been along here that, following the Heiji Rebellion, Minamoto Yoshitomo and his sons had sought to escape the wrath of Taira Kiyomori by scaling the southern slopes of Mount Ibuki in the midst of winter. And it had been here, too, that Oda Nobunaga, having first subdued Gifu Castle, had defeated the Miyoshi and Kitabatake forces, opening up the way to the capital and the Home Provinces.

It is no weather to lift the spirits when Ieyasu dismounts from his horse and strides up to his tent to receive the first reports from his commanders in the field. It is fall, the time of year when fierce typhoons sweep in from the southern Pacific to hit the Japanese islands with their relentless force. It seems that this is exactly what lies in store for the gathered warriors, for the wind is picking up fast and already a thick veil of rain hangs over the landscape, subduing the vivid colors of their armor, the silk banners, and the bright sparkle of the long lances. The air of gloom among the eastern warriors is lifted as if by magic when Ieyasu's messengers report that all of the enemy forces are still stationed near Ōgaki Castle, just south-east of them, leaving unprotected the two-mile-wide strip of land that runs westward toward the old barrier town of Sekigahara.

The news seems too good to be true. Sekigahara's geographic position is just too important to leave unguarded. From here the massive Ibuki Mountains range northward, all the way north to Tsuruga, where they plummet into Tsuruga Bay. Southward from Sekigahara run the Yōrō Mountains, an equally long and impenetrable stretch of mountains, right into the heart of the mountainous Ise Peninsula. Situated at the point where both ranges meet, Sekigahara is the gateway between eastern and western Japan.

How can it be that Mitsunari has not seized his advantage? Is it that, as a descendant of western warlords, who have always had unhampered access to the Home Provinces, he does not appreciate the barrier's historic importance? Or is it something else? Is it perhaps the weather? It certainly appears that the unrelenting rain has gotten to Mitsunari's troops, for Ieyasu's scouts can detect no exceptional movements among them, even after his arrival that afternoon. Only a small group of mounted warriors have loomed up out of the haze to harass his troops stationed along the Makuse River. It is no more than a provocation, and the dreary day draws to a miserable close without any further engagements.

That same evening Ieyasu convenes a council of all his commanders in the field. The next day, he tells them, they will press on westward and try to pass the ancient barrier. They will leave behind some five thousand men, far too few to defeat the enemy, but enough to keep them preoccupied for the remainder to pass the barrier into Ōmi province. From there they will march on the castles of Sawayama, Fushimi, and Osaka, the centers of western opposition.

Ieyasu (right) and his generals share some *sake* on the eve of battle

Early on the morning of October 21, Ieyasu is woken with worrying news from two messengers, one from Fukushima Masanori and one from Nishio Mitsunori. It seems that during the previous evening, while Ieyasu and his generals were mapping out their strategy for the next day, a huge contingent of Mitsunari's army has broken camp at Ōgaki and begun to march westward, straight to the plains of Sekigahara. Caught in a blinding rainstorm they temporarily lost their way, but shortly after midnight, they reached the foot of Mount Sasao, where they have now taken up positions on high ground. For a moment it seems that Ieyasu has been masterfully outwitted. The mounted warriors who came down from Ōgaki to harass his soldiers the previous day were no more than a decoy to distract the attention of his scouts from the larger troop movements farther afield.

Troop placement in the early stages of the battle: Ieyasu's camp is in the bottom right panel. Kuroda Nagamasa's camp (marked by blue banners) is at the top of the second panel from the right, while Fukushima Masanori and Honda Tadakatsu (with red banners) have taken up positions at the bottom edge of the third panel from the right. Immediately behind them are those of Tanaka Yoshimasa. Ishida Mitsunari's camp (with white banners) is at the top of the third panel from the right. In the bottom left-hand panel, on the southern bank of the Imasu River, are the forces of Kobayakawa Hideaki. At the top of the third panel from the left are Ukita Hideie and his men, their blue banners clearly visible. Just below are those of Shimazu Yoshihiro, who is also part of the western alliance.

Ueda Castle, an unnecessary diversion

It seems Ieyasu has underestimated Mitsunari. Now the latter clearly has the advantage: he has blocked off the barrier and occupies high ground. It seems that his forces are in the majority, too, albeit by a narrow margin. Of all these setbacks it is the last one that irks Ieyasu the most. It should have been the other way round! Close to forty thousand more troops have taken the inland route along the Nakasendō under the command of his son, Hidetada. Given that Hidetada departed from Utsunomiya on the first of October—a week before he himself departed from Edo—those troops should long since have arrived in Mino. Lines of communication along the inland route are poor, and the last news he has had from his son is that he is tied down in Shinano, where he has laid siege to Ueda Castle. It is an unnecessary diversion. Ueda Castle does not lie along the Nakasendō, but along a side road, into Echigo and the northwestern provinces.

The seasoned commander soon recovers from the setback. Rising from his field bed, he immediately begins to issue orders. All troops are to im-

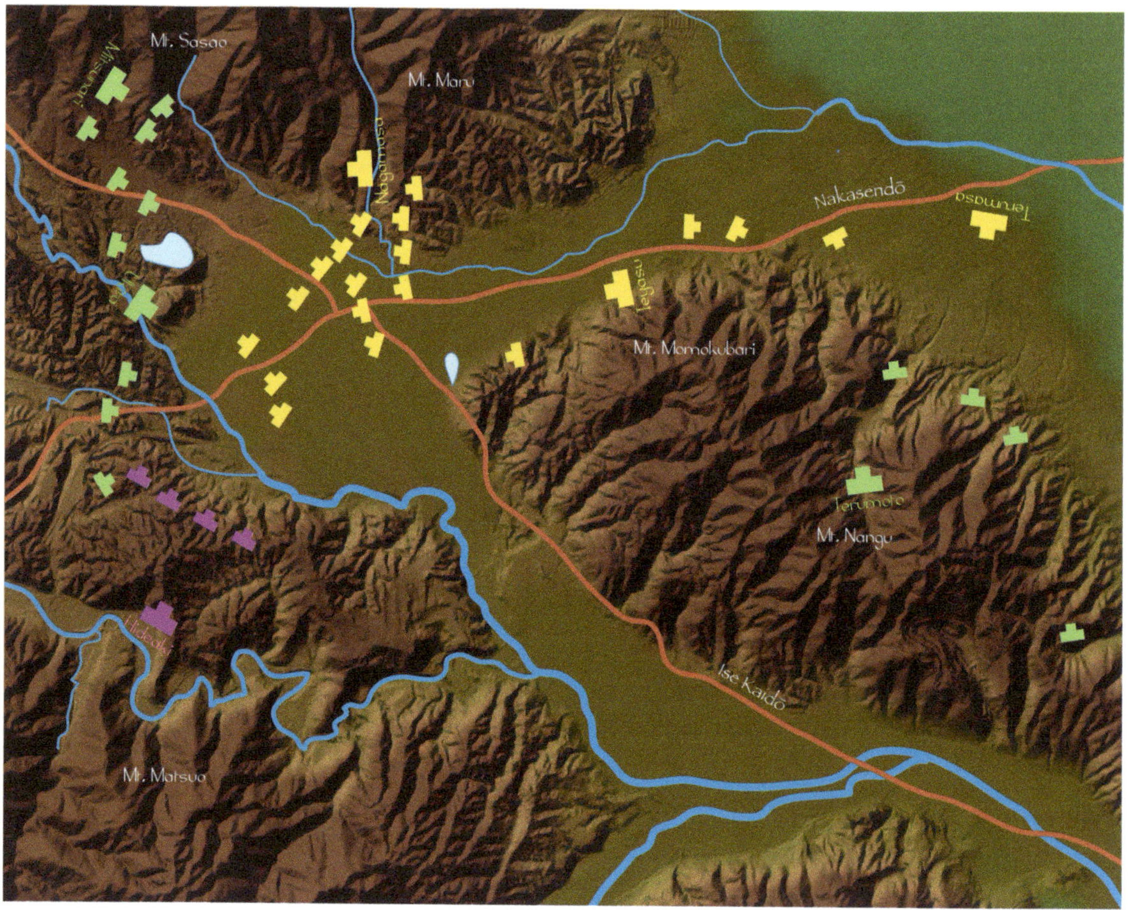

mediately march on Sekigahara and position themselves opposite the western forces as best they can. He himself will follow with his own force of thirty thousand men. Only Ikeda Terumasa and his men are to remain behind to cover the rear. Not all of Mitsunari's allies might yet have departed from Ōgaki and if they are quick they might still be able to cut them off from Mitsunari's advance force. But on their way, they run into such dense fog that Ieyasu is forced to halt his troops for fear of losing his way, and to wait until the clouds lift.

It is five o'clock in the morning when Ieyasu sets up his field headquarters at the foot of Mount Momokubari and that his twenty contingents take up their positions on the low-lying fields below the enemy positions. By that time the brunt of the western force had positioned themselves on high ground around the Ikedera pond. Only a few of their contingents, among them those of Mōri Hidemoto, Kikkawa Hiroie, and Natsuka Masaie have lagged behind, but they too have taken up positions on high ground, a few miles south to where Ikeda's men are stationed.

By eight o'clock, the unrelenting rain of the previous night has somewhat lessened. Shrouds of mist still linger on the low-lying plain, but the troops are so closely dispersed in the narrow valley that many, including those of the enemy, are still visible through the haze. It seems as if the whole valley is alive with movement as close to two hundred thousand warriors ready themselves for the moment of truth. Facing the western troops at the center of the plain are the Hosokawa, the Katō, the Nagaoka. Beyond them, at the foot of Mount Maru, are the forces of Kuroda Nagamasa, right opposite those of Mitsunari, at the foot of Mount Sasao.

It is more by impulse than by design that, on the morning of October 21, the first shots ring out across the plains of Sekigahara. At less than a mile, the troops of Fukushima Masanori are closest to the enemy. It is a position to be envied. If they survive, it will be they who are the first to take the head of an enemy. That head will immediately be sent back to Ieyasu for inspection

The opening volleys of the Battle of Sekigahara

and be declared the ichiban kubi, the first enemy head to be taken in battle. Needless to say that such a feat will be copiously rewarded after the battle. But Masanori sees his chances go up in smoke when, shortly after eight o'-clock, a small group of mounted warriors carrying Matsudaira and Ii banners detach themselves from the rear and forces their way through the gap between his ranks and those of the Tanaka and Tsutsui. They are led by Ieyasu's fourth son, Matsudaira Tadayoshi, seconded by Ii Naomasa. Their sudden action causes a great degree of consternation among the commanders in the front line, especially Fukushima Masanori. For no sooner has the contingent entered no man's land, than they swerve left—straight into Masanori's line of attack—heading straight for the Ukita and Shimazu banners in the enemy line. Fearing that they are stealing a march on him, Masanori loses his temper and orders his riflemen to open fire. The fire is immediately answered by the other side, causing the horsemen to be caught in the crossfire. Within

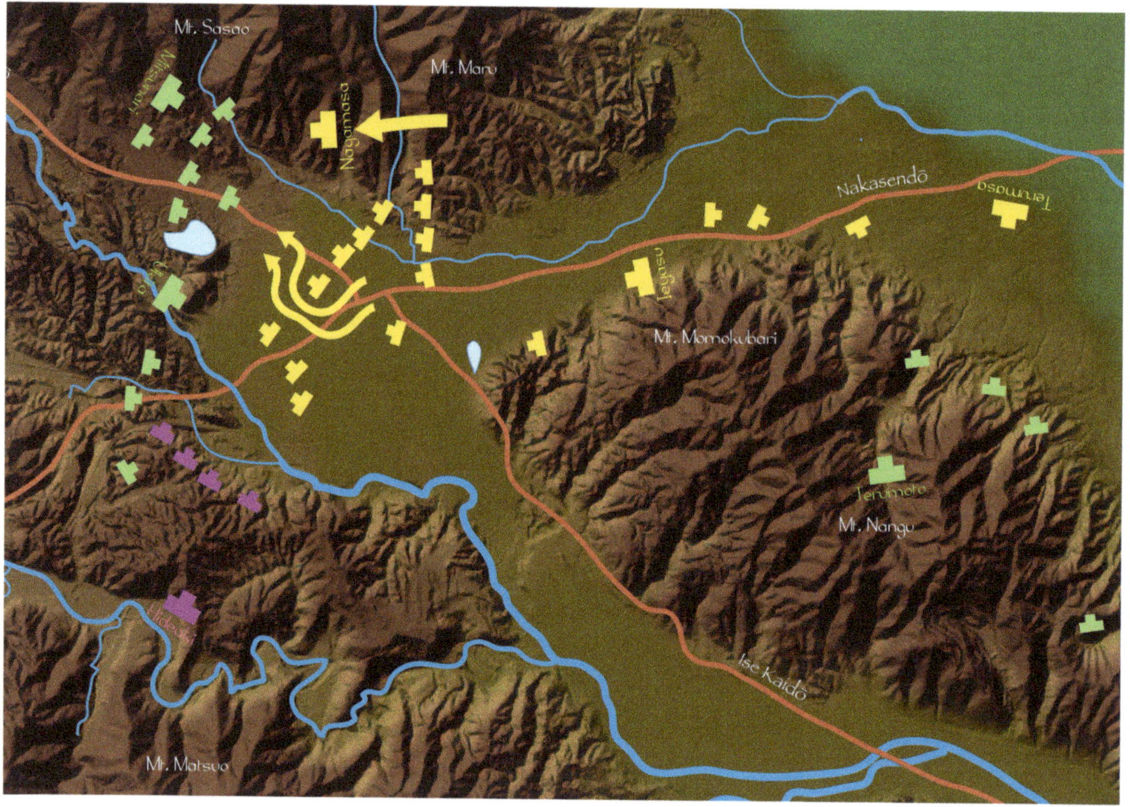

Fukushima Masanori in the heat of battle

moments of the first exchange of volleys a thin plume of smoke begins to climb skyward from the foot of Mount Maru, signaling that, forced by the short temper of his commanders, Kuroda Nagamasa has given orders to commence overall hostilities. The battle of Sekigahara had begun in earnest.

Spotting the signal fires on their right, all the commanders along the front line now order their musketeers to open fire. Thick plumes of smoke belch forth from the arrayed muzzles to mingle with the heavy morning air so that within moments the thin stretch of land between the two armies is covered by a dense layer of smog. Then, after several volleys have been exchanged, Tsutsui Sadatsugu orders his musketeers to stand aside and let a phalanx of spearmen advance.

Opposition is fierce, especially from the Ukita and Konishi warriors, whose total number is close to twenty thousand. They fight with such determination that by eleven o'clock the eastern forces are pushed back beyond the positions from which they advanced three hours before. Worried by the way the battle is going, even Ieyasu has become restless, leaving his camp at the foot of Mount Momokubari to take up position at the center of the plain, right behind his forces. But the stalemate continues so that by noon there is no way to tell which way the pendulum will swing.

太平記拾遺
金吾
中納言秀秋
十九

Opposite page: Kobayakawa Hideaki, the western warlord who defected to Ieyasu's side

Mitsunari, too, has begun to lose patience. He sends up smoke signals, urging those commanders who have not yet joined the battle to do so. The most important of these are Mōri Terumoto and Kobayakawa Hideaki. The former, who is still facing the Ikeda contingent from Mount Nangu, now finds himself cut off by his vassal Kikkawa Hiroie, who has been persuaded by Ieyasu to change sides in exchange for his lord's domains. Hideaki, who has taken up positions on Mount Matsuo, toward the south of the scene of battle, also fails to move. On the eve of battle, he promised Mitsunari to join the fight on the latter's signal and attack Ieyasu's forces from the rear. But even when Mitsunari sends a messenger over to Mount Matsuo with an urgent request for assistance Hideaki refuses to budge.

Spotting the smoke signal, Ieyasu has a good idea of why Hideaki is reluctant to move. While still at Edo Castle, Hideaki sent him a long letter apologizing for the fall of Fushimi Castle, professing that circumstances forced him to participate in the castle's siege. Seeking to capitalize on Hideaki's sense of guilt, Ieyasu too has sent missives to Mount Matsuo, but they have all come back without any firm commitments: the young warlord

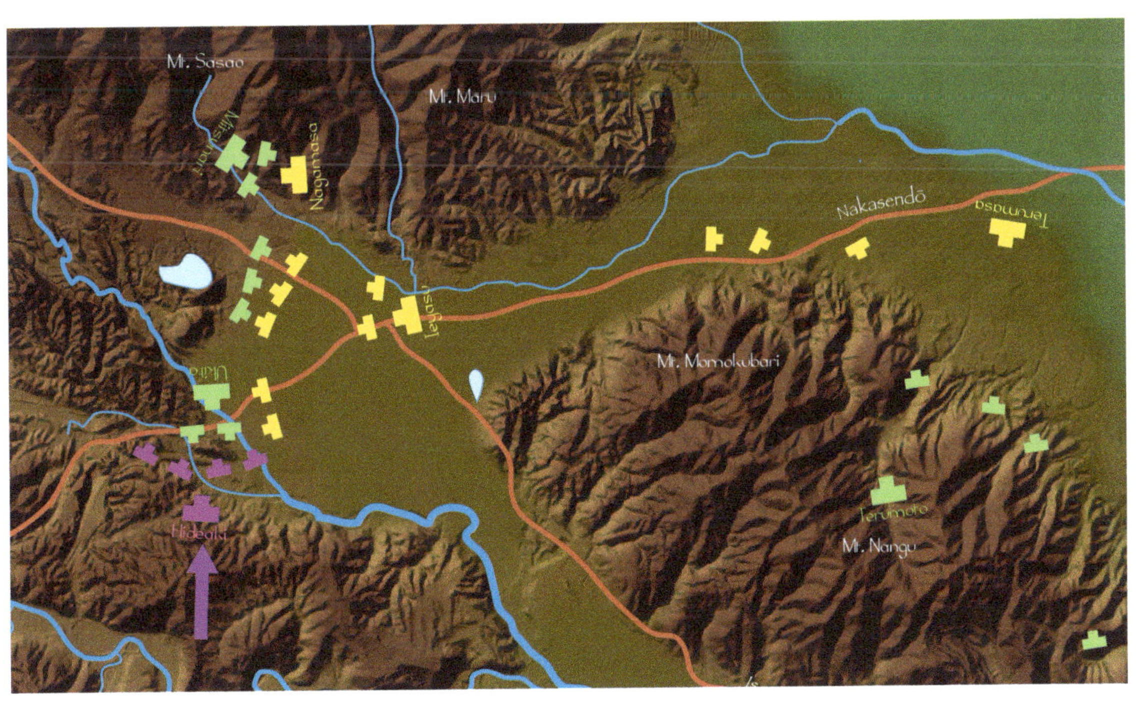

The effect of Hideaki's defection is almost instantaneous

is obviously torn by conflicting emotions. What is needed is a good prodding, something to stimulate his senses. And thus, without hesitating, Ieyasu orders his men to open fire on Hideaki's troops, hoping to thereby jolt the young warrior into declaring himself. Almost immediately Ieyasu's genius for reading men's minds reveals itself. As if roused from a slumber, the young warlord stands up in his stirrups, points his battle fan in the direction of the western Otani forces and orders his men to 'aim for the Otani ranks.'

The effect of Hideaki's defection is almost instantaneous. The eastern warriors, worn down by the repeated setbacks over the previous hours, find new courage as they observe how Kobayakawa's six thousand warriors rush down the slopes of Mount Matsuo and begin to attack the Ōtani and Toda troops, who are now wedged between the huge Ukita force and the foot of the mountain. Thus far all of them have bravely withstood the continued assault, but now they begin to lose the will to fight, as they find themselves confronted by an army refreshed and superior in numbers. Through superhuman effort they repel the first attack, driving Hideaki's men back up the mountain's slopes, but then disaster strikes as four other eastern commanders who have taken up positions at the foot of the mountain also change sides and order their men to join those of Hideaki. Under these enormous

Opposite page: Kobayakawa Hideaki, haunted by the ghosts of those he betrayed

魁題百撰相
一魁斎芳年筆
金吾 中納言秀秋

pressures the Ōtani and Toda ranks gradually begin to collapse, until those who are still standing begin to retreat northward, into the ranks of the Ukita, and then those of the Konishi. Before long they, too, are overwhelmed by the two-pronged assault.

It is with a sinking feeling that Mitsunari watches the remnants of the Ukita and Konishi regiments, the largest he has put in the field, now run past him, blooded, disheveled, disheartened. It is not their lack of valor that has lost him his victory, but the failure of the others to come to their rescue: the Mōri, the Natsuka, the Ankokuji, the Shimazu—all of them stand by idly as their allies are being butchered in the thousands. In the end, Mitsunari too deserts his allies. One final time he issues a command to his troops, this time to pack up and retreat west along the Hokkoku Kaidō. It is two o'clock. The fighting will go on till late in the afternoon, but Mitsunari's flight confirms that the outcome of the battle has been decided.

Following his flight from the scene of battle, Mitsunari makes his way to the village of Furuhashi along the Takatoki River. There the *ochimusha* steals a boat from a local fisherman and rows upstream to find shelter among the snow-clad slopes of the Ibuki Mountains. When he is finally captured, he is found cowering in a cave, suffering from cold and hunger. Two weeks later, on November 6, he is beheaded at the Rokujōgawara, the ancient execution grounds on the banks of the Kamo River in Kyoto.

Ieyasu's victory at Sekigahara is a decisive blow to the western alliance. It is not the final defeat of the pro-Toyotomi forces; that will come fourteen years later, in the winter and summer sieges of Osaka Castle. But it is enough for Ieyasu to pronounce himself Seiitai Shōgun and establish the Tokugawa shogunate, which will rule over a peaceful nation for close to three centuries.

GLOSSARY

ashigaru: Foot soldier.

Bakufu: Military, lit. 'tent,' government.

bugyō: Magistrate.

dōmaru: Harness or 'body wrap.' The whole harness, including the breastplate, was made of small scales of hard leather or metal laced into plates by means of cord and lacquered.

genpuku: Coming-of-age ceremony.

Go-Bugyō: Council of (five) Commissioners.

Go-Tairō: Council of (five) Regents.

hatamoto: Direct retainer, or "bannerman," of the *Shōgun*.

igo: Game based on capturing territory.

jinjiro: Makeshift bastion.

kaishaku: The assistant (often a confidant) who cuts off someone's head the moment he has plunged his dagger into his lower abdomen.

kubi jikken: Inspection of the severed heads of the enemy warriors.

mikuji: Fortune slip.

ochimusha:	Defeated warriors fleeing the scene of battle.
otona hyakushō:	Armed peasants
ronkōkōshō:	Formal occasion in which a lord rewards his retainers.
sake:	Rice wine.
seppuku:	Ritual suicide in which a person plunged his dagger into his lower abdomen.
Shōgun:	Hereditary military governor during Japan's fuedal era.
taigi meibun:	A 'just cause' for which to go into battle.
taikō:	Drum.
Taikō-sama:	Honorary name specifically used for Toyotomi Hideyoshi.
tekkōsen:	Ironclad.
Tenka-dono:	Honorary name specifically used for Tokugawa Ieyasu.
tenka fūbū:	Rule the entire realm (by force).
teppō bugyō:	Magistrate of muskets.
tomurai kassen:	'Memorial battle' in honor of one's defeated lord.
yama:	Mountain or hill.
yari:	Lance.
yashiki:	Samurai mansion.
yoriki:	Chief of police.
wakizashi:	Dagger.

INDEX

IN THE SAME SERIES

SAMURAI SIEGES

THE LONG ROAD TO UNIFICATION

WILLIAM DE LANGE

TOYO PRess publishes books that contribute to a deeper understanding of Asian cultures. Book and cover design: Chōkei Studios. Printing and binding: IngramSpark. The typefaces are Purloin, Futurist, and Marcellus.

www.ingramcontent.com/pod-product-compliance
Ingram Content Group UK Ltd.
Pitfield, Milton Keynes, MK11 3LW, UK
UKHW061952290726
14090UKWH00021B/1188